Kingdom Encounters

"And I will give you the keys of the kingdom of heaven, and whatever you bind on earth will be bound in heaven, and whatever you loose on earth will be loosed in heaven."
~Matthew 16:9

* * *

"Your kingdom come. Your will be done on earth as it is in heaven."
~Matthew 6:10

* * *

"From that time Jesus began to preach and to say, 'Repent, for the kingdom of heaven is at hand.'"
~Matthew 4:17

* * *

"In Him all the treasures of [divine] wisdom (comprehensive insight into the ways and purposes of God) and [all the riches of spiritual] knowledge and enlightenment are stored up."
~Colossians 2:3 (AMP)

Kingdom Encounters

Keys to Unlocking God's Treasures

By

Jay W. West

and

Jason B. West

7710-T Cherry Park Dr., Suite 224

Houston, Texas 77095

Kingdom Encounters

Copyright © 2014 by Jay W. West

Anointed 2 Go MdM
Bellevue, NE

Cover & Key Images © Copyright byDesign 2014, Cynthia Pleskac

All rights reserved. This book is protected by the copyright laws of the United States of America. This book or any parts therein may not be reproduced, distributed, copied or transmitted in any form, not electronic, mechanical or any other means, or stored in a database or retrieval system without the prior written permission of the publisher. The use of short quotations or occasional passage copying for personal or group study is permitted and encouraged.

Unless otherwise identified, all Scripture quotations are from the New King James Version. Copyright © 1982 by Thomas Nelson, Inc. Used by permission. All rights reserved.

Scripture quotations marked (AMP) or "The Amplified Bible" are taken from THE AMPLIFIED BIBLE. Old Testament copyright © 1965, 1987 by The Zondervan Corporation. The Amplified New Testament copyright © 1958, 1987 by The Lockman Foundation. Used by permission.

Scripture quotations marked (KJV) or "King James Version" are taken from the King James Version of the Bible. Public domain.

Scripture quotations marked (NASB) or "New American Standard Bible" are taken from the NEW AMERICAN STANDARD BIBLE®, Copyright © 1960, 1962, 1963, 1968, 1971, 1972, 1973, 1975, 1977, 1995 by The Lockman Foundation. Used by permission.

Scripture quotations marked (MSG) or "The Message Bible" are taken from THE MESSAGE. Copyright © 1993, 1994, 1995, 1996, 2000, 2001, 2002. Used by permission of NavPress Publishing Group.

Scripture quotations marked (VOICE) or "The Voice" are taken from *The Voice Bible* Copyright © 2012 Thomas Nelson, Inc. The Voice™ translation © 2012 Ecclesia Bible Society.

Ebook: 978-1-304-83362-4
Paperback: 978-1-365-73863-0
Hardcover: 978-1-304-83361-7

Table of Contents

Dedication 7

Acknowledgments 9

Foreword By Jack Taylor 13

Introduction By Jason West 17

Chapter One The Royal Flush 21

Chapter Two The Tractor and the Rattlesnake 39

Chapter Three Prison Break-In—Getting Cheesed 55

Chapter Four Anointed Afterglow 75

Chapter Five Praying the Price in Public 93

Chapter Six The Un-Young Renewed Youth Minister 109

Chapter Seven WOW! WOW! WOW! 127

Chapter Eight Prepare for the Arrival of Revival 145

Chapter Nine Prayer Encounters By Jason West 161

Notes 173

Kingdom Encounters

Dedication

I dedicate this book to two husband and wife teams that I have seen grow significantly in their faith, respond to God's call, and then initiate new ministries as a result.

The first couple is John and Helen Weesner from Sugar Land, Texas. I initially met John and Helen back in 1984 very near the beginning of my nine years of ministry at Faith Lutheran Church, where I was called to serve in the areas of evangelism, administration, prayer, and discipleship. I remember awkwardly sitting across from them at a luncheon of some sort, and we were all trying to figure out what to say to each other. At the time, John and Helen were nominal churchgoers, but over the years, I watched with amazement as they encountered Jesus at so many junctures, in so many places, with great enthusiasm and eagerness that would have startled most people. I think even the angels noticed this one. In fact, I know they did because I saw an angel at their home one evening.

John and Helen added many different ministry elements to their growth patterns, including but not limited to early morning-prayer, preschool teaching, worship leading, evangelism and administration boards, participating in prison ministry, and ultimately meeting Chuck Colson. They also hosted one of the fastest growing and most anointed home ministry groups in our church. In addition, they went on a year-long mission trip to Venezuela, followed by shorter ones, all in what would be normal retirement ages too. They are the real deal when it comes to authentic Christians who believe in the power of God for today. I am blessed to call them friends.

The second couple is Steve and Cindy Hittle from Lighthouse Fellowship in Hugoton, Kansas, where I was the senior pastor for several years. Steve and Cindy were pretty much hometown rural folks who rarely ventured too far away from their small town responsibilities, except for an occasional vacation or work-related trip. I had to work hard to get them to travel to Florida to attend the revival in Pensacola. However, that one trip somehow sparked their enthusiasm and opened their eyes to what God could do and wanted to do in other parts of the country and the world. Since then, they have traveled and ministered in these countries: Tanzania (2001), Trinidad/Tobago (2002), Turkey (2007), Uganda (2009), Peru (2009), Kenya (2011), Israel (2012), and Mexico (2014). Plus, they have been serving as interim pastors at their church for nearly two years.

Additionally, they serve in their community on the city council and at the public library, often providing food and housing for others and sharing Jesus with so many people. Steve and Cindy are anointed and amazing, and I love their zeal, tenacity, and faithfulness to those tasks that God continues to give them.

I count it a joy to know both of these couples and to see them continue to flow with more and more Kingdom Encounters. They both soak in the fresh anointing of God and then squeeze it out to others in ways that promote and enhance the lives of those they reach out to. I am honored to count them as ministry partners for the good of the Kingdom, for the sake of a fallen world, and for the love of Jesus!

Acknowledgments

Father God, Jesus, and the Holy Spirit: Thank You for the Word of God, Your love, salvation, and anointing, all of which contribute to powerful personal Kingdom Encounters.

Diane West: Thank you for your love, patience, support, and encouragement! These thirty-five years of marriage have undoubtedly been the best years of my life. God brought you to me as a taste of why a Kingdom Encounter is so important! You are a great representative portraying the virtuous wife outlined in Proverbs 31. Your Kingdom life depicts and manifests loving Kingdom Encounters, and I am the honored recipient of those encounters. When I think of a Kingdom Encounter, I think of Diane West, who graciously, with mercy, peace, and kindness, proves over and over to me that I am indeed a very blessed man.

Jason West: Thank you for your love, amazing writing and editing skills, along with your confidence. You are the best worship leader I know. You are anointed, talented, and gifted. To have you coauthor this book is a delight that I shall cherish the rest of my life. Let's do it again soon!

Pastor Jack Taylor: A thank-you does not seem adequate, but it is heartfelt and deeply appreciated. I am so glad we met you back in the 1980s, and more recently that you agreed to write the foreword for this work, along with giving your endorsement of *Willing to Yield*. I am thrilled to know you and can't wait to see what God does with you next. It is going to be outstanding! Until then, let's sing in His reign.

Gary Peterson: This is the third book you have edited for me. Your skill, enthusiasm, humor, and expertise are sincerely appreciated and definitely one of the best around. I believe I owe you some bear claws.

Pastor Jim Hart: Five years under your ministry have now produced four books and one worship album in our family. Not to mention numerous faith-filled acquisitions, all of which I believe are a direct influence from your personal "tell it like it is" preaching. This, coupled with your anointed prayers and pastoral kindness, along with personal encouragement and friendship, have produced eternal benefits. Praise God for your faithfulness!

Cynthia Pleskac: Once again, you have come through with an amazing artistic cover design that displays your wonderful standard of excellence. I am thrilled that you worked with me on this project and hope it continues for many years to come. Your cover design renders exactly what I wanted to convey. Thanks so much!

A note from Jason West:

The process of designing, crafting, and publishing this book has truly been a privilege and an honor for me. I, too, want to express my sincere gratitude to those who were involved in this process. I echo my dad's acknowledgments to those listed above. May your diligence and dedication prove to be an investment that will cause you to reap great Kingdom rewards.

Thanks be to God, who has given us the ideas, inspiration, and initiative to complete this task. Lord, take this book and use it for Your glory to promote Kingdom Encounters in the lives of all who read it.

*Please note: This book has undergone two critical editing reviews, in which two different trained editors have thoroughly commented, critiqued, and corrected all the errors they could find. In addition to those reviews, I (Jay) personally reexamined and

Acknowledgements

inspected the book several times for final polishing. However, despite our best efforts, we admit that catching every typo and every grammatical error is a very difficult, tedious, and time-consuming task to accomplish. We have done our best, but please be gracious if you still find an occasional lingering discrepancy. Thank you.

Foreword
By Jack Taylor

When I began to read this book, I became suddenly aware that it was remarkable in many ways. The best way for me to respond to it is to report to the reader of its effects on me personally. For many years I have been studying the all-important issue of the Kingdom of God. Early on in my study I was stricken with its immensity, its ultimacy, and its indispensable influence on everything we believe. I have plans to write a book on the subject and am moved when a book like this comes along. It is not a theological treatise but an exercise in what I call practical "Kingdomology." It is not about the Kingdom, but about the Kingdom's influence when it is practiced and applied. It is an easy read because it chronicles a lifestyle of continuity regarding the "at hand" Kingdom. My sevenfold response follows:

> **1. I am intrigued.** What intrigues me the most is a constant attention given to the nearness of the spiritual realm and how it is possible to draw not only from the riches of the Kingdom of God but to operate in its power. Paul said it best when he remarked, "The Kingdom of God is not a matter of talk but of power" (1 Corinthians 4:20). Power is the capacity to affect change. When the Kingdom of God meets the realities of the worldly realm, the Kingdom wins.

> **2. I am hopeful.** This is the story of a man who has discovered the Kingdom and operates daily in expectation that it can be experienced and encountered. I am driven by such a discovery, which, when experienced

by all of us, will spark revival fires that cannot be stopped. I believe we are in that season when God is moving to restore Kingdom mentality to the weakened church, bringing the church out of its self-absorption into Kingdom-centeredness.

3. I am encouraged. The simplicity of the presentation of the Kingdom of God in action leaves no argument that withstands the reality of God's rule (i.e., Kingdom). When an issue becomes complicated, we run across the footprints of the devil. It's simple: "God rules! Embrace it. Declare it. Release it!" That encourages me.

4. I am challenged. I have been confronted by my own failures to be constantly aware of the presence of the Kingdom and its eternal relevance amid the frustrations and hurts of this world. I am urged by this work to allow God to make me alert that there are more people around me seeking for the Kingdom and who are eager to share the riches of the Kingdom.

5. I am committed. At a new level, I desire to allow God to "Kingdomize" me to the extent that I cannot open my mouth without releasing the Kingdom. It becomes obvious even to the casual reader of the New Testament that this was the simple protocol in the ministry of Jesus; namely to watch God work and join Him and listen to God speak and speak it.

6. I am excited! I am seeing the Kingdom of God move from a concept, a point of theology, to a lifestyle of practice. The world will be aroused to faith when we transition the message of the Kingdom to the transcendent power embodied in it.

7. I am yielded! At the ripe age of eighty, I am becoming increasingly aware that we do not have the ultimate truth as God wants us to have it until we learn to release it in practical living. If the world could be saved by sermons, we would have accomplished that long ago. The cultures of the world can only be changed by the ultimate, eternal, and unshakable Kingdom of God borne through the lives of Kingdom citizens.

Jay and Jason, thank you for this unique presentation of the Kingdom in action. I pray for this book to have a wide reading and a long life as a text of continuing proof that the Kingdom of God is at hand!

This work deserves to be read again and again to sensitize us to the relevance, reality and practice of God's eternal government as a lifestyle of believers all over the world!

I predict this book will have a long and fruitful life.

"And the Gospel of the Kingdom will be preached in the whole world as a testimony to all nations, and then the end shall come" (Matthew 24:14).

Jack Taylor, President
Dimensions Ministries
Melbourne, Florida
http://www.jackrtaylor.com

Introduction
By Jason West

"Your kingdom come. Your will be done on earth as it is in heaven."
~Matt. 6:10

The above verse, taken from the Lord's Prayer, is perhaps the most clear and succinct description in the Bible of what a Kingdom Encounter is. It involves God's Kingdom coming and encountering the earth, causing things on earth to become as they are in heaven. It is the believers' mandate to pray for Kingdom Encounters to happen on this earth on a regular basis. Yet, what exactly does such an encounter look like? That is what this book endeavors to describe.

Interestingly enough, one of the antonyms for the word *encounter* in Webster's thesaurus is the word *yielding*. Now, this may not seem to bear too much significance, except for the fact that the previous book my father, Jay West, wrote is entitled *Willing to Yield*. Now, he is writing about the opposite of yielding, which is encountering. Is this contradictory? Absolutely not. It is simply two sides of the same coin. Let me explain: We do the yielding, and God does the encountering. When we yield to God, we can expect Him to respond to that yielding process by encountering us with His Kingdom. Experiencing a Kingdom encounter can only happen when we have hearts that have yielded to Him. If you want to know more about yielding, you're encouraged to pick up a copy of *Willing to Yield* and to be blessed by reading it for yourself! The title of this book came into existence as a result of a series of home fellowship meetings my family hosted for about a year and a half, which we entitled Kingdom Encounters. These meetings were biweekly times in which people would gather in our house and experience an encounter with the Kingdom of God through worship, deep Bible study, prayer ministry, and fellowship with other believers. Many people came through our doors at various times throughout this year and a half journey with the simple desire to experience God in a deeper, fuller, and more meaningful way than they had up to that point in their lives. After hosting this group for quite some time, we decided there should be a book written about this topic.

Of course, this book is not just about the Kingdom Encounters that we hosted in our home. It contains testimonies from all kinds of life experiences and situations, focusing on the diversity of ways God desires to encounter us with His Kingdom. Kingdom Encounters with God come in many forms, including evangelism, discipleship, worship, financial blessing, healing, and a number of other topics that will be covered throughout this book.

An encounter is a life-changing moment in which circumstances meet face-to-face with destiny to produce an ever-increasing, all-encompassing transformational work within us. God is the God of encounters. One of the things God does best is to invade our schedules and change our lives if we are willing to yield and to allow Him to encounter us. When we pray and contend for a move of God in our lives, He responds by encountering us in a strong, dynamic way. Yet, in spite of our prayers and our efforts to press in, we still are often surprised when the encounter happens! This is because encounters do not always come at times when we expect them. Yet, God always encounters us at just the right time. Encounters are God-breathed, God-ordained, and intended for our benefit! God *is* the God of encounters. He encountered Jacob through a wrestling match. He encountered Moses with a burning bush. He encountered Paul with His marvelous light. And I believe He wants to encounter you too if you will have a heart willing to allow God to invade. Encounters are the *kairos* moments of God—

the set times when He chooses to interfere with mankind for His sovereign purposes.

When I think of encounters, one of the first things that comes to mind is the account of Jacob's wrestling encounter with God, found in Genesis 32:22–32. In this passage, Jacob was faced with the imminence of meeting his estranged brother Esau face-to-face. Because of the ways he had deceived Esau in the past (stealing Esau's birthright and his firstborn blessing), he fully expected Esau still to be seeking to kill him. However, what Jacob did not expect was that, the night before he met Esau, a Man would encounter him and wrestle with him until daybreak. This was not just any Man; this was the Angel of the LORD.

Many biblical scholars agree that the capital "A" Angel of the LORD is an appearance of God the Son in Old Testament times. This appearance of God in the flesh is known as a *theophany*. Throughout the Old Testament, the times when God showed up in human form and encountered His people in some way are known as theophany moments. They are moments when God interrupted human daily life to offer something new and something different to behold. Similar theophany encounters in the Bible include when the Angel of the LORD blocked the roadway in front of Balaam's donkey (Num. 22:22–38); when the Angel of the LORD spoke to Gideon and called him a "mighty man of valor" (Jdg. 6:11–23); and when the Angel of the LORD appeared to Manoah and his wife, giving them specific instructions for how to raise their soon-coming child named Samson (Jdg. 13:3–22). Additionally, the Angel of the LORD is also found appearing to Hagar, Abraham, Moses, and the entire nation of Israel.

In the Old Testament, theophanies were encounters in which God came to be with man for a specific reason. Yet, in the New Testament, we find that Jesus is *Immanuel*, which means, "God with us" (Matt. 1:23). Thus, under the New Covenant, every day with God should be a theophany encounter. Bill Johnson has been quoted as saying that Bible knowledge without Bible experience is pointless. This is a valid statement, indeed. Theology sets the biblical foundation for knowledge about God, but it is the daily experience of His theophany encounters that take us from knowledge to experience.

That's what a Kingdom Encounter is all about. It's about creating a culture in which wrestling with God is the norm. Let me explain. Jacob wrestled with God for a blessing that he previously tried to gain through deception, lying, and cheating. But when God encountered him, Jacob knew that only God could truly bestow the blessing that He so desired. And this time, Jacob was determined to receive the blessing "fair and square." He did not cheat his way through, but he wrestled with God until daybreak, not letting Him go until God blessed him. When God finally blessed him, He also gave him a new name. He went from being *Jacob*, which means "deceiver" and "one who grasps at another's heels," to *Israel*, which means "one who struggled with God and prevailed." In essence, Jacob went from being defeated to being an overcomer—from being a heel to being a healer. He had a Kingdom encounter with God that he would never forget.

I believe that God desires that we would enjoy daily Kingdom Encounters with Him—daily theophany experiences in which knowledge and experience come together to produce wonderful fruit in our lives for His Kingdom. As you go through life, and even as you read this book, you will likely find yourself wrestling with God at times. The question is: What are you wrestling for? A blessing? A breakthrough? A life-changing encounter that leaves you considerably different than you were before? I tell you, yes, all these things are enwrapped in what the experience of a Kingdom Encounter is all about. Are you willing to press in for such an encounter? If so, pray this simple prayer with me: "Your kingdom come. Your will be done on earth as it is in heaven" (Matt. 6:10). May His Kingdom continue to encounter this earth both now and evermore. Amen.

Chapter One

The Royal Flush

Back in 1983, my wife Diane and I were invited to move from the Midwest to minister at Calvary Lutheran in Charleston, South Carolina. Upon arriving, the senior pastor, Robert Duddleston, began sharing with us about something he called the "Infilling of the Holy Spirit" or the "Baptism of the Holy Spirit." To be honest, initially I really had no idea what he was talking about, nor did I really care. That sounds harsh and maybe cruel, but it is the truth. In fact, I remember actually and brazenly telling him that I would take care of the traditional crowd and he could handle the more Spirit-filled crowd. That was a very arrogant response for which I have repented, but at the time it was reality.

If I had been more spiritually mature, I could have easily recognized that this was a setup by God for our future and for the ministry in which we now engage, but my eyes were dimmed by human deception, simply because I was in a hard place at the time.

The previous year to coming to South Carolina, we were in what I would describe as an abusive pastoral position. Let me explain. If I did something wrong in my former church, I was brought into the pastor's office where he would cuss and swear, being intimidating and dominating in his approach to correction. During the worship services he would sit off to the side in a small room and smoke, only coming out when it was his turn to do something. There is more that I could share, but suffice it to say that it was a difficult year. So when we decided to put our name out, showing availability for a new position, and this life-giving man of God approached us from South Carolina, I should have recognized that this was God's rescue plan.

In preparation for our move, I told the Lord in prayer that if this particular church did not work out, then I was going to resign from the ministry and go into some other line of work because my frustration level was high, and I was tired of being chewed on and spit out like some sort of bad taste in your mouth. Ministry was losing its fun and life-giving edge for me, and I was definitely ready for something new, exciting, and at least some place where I could be treated as a good person.

This particular Lutheran church in South Carolina was known as a Spirit-filled Lutheran church. I know that is an oxymoron for some, but it was the truth. To be very honest, I do not know why they selected me, other than to say it had to be a God thing. For you see, they had three candidates, two of them already flowing with and enjoying the benefits of being in a Spirit-filled environment, and then there was me. And for some reason they picked me. Can you imagine God and this church making that mistake? (smile)

Anyway, after a few months in this church, I approached Diane and asked her why we did not want to enter into this thing called the "Infilling of the Holy Spirit" or "Baptism of the Holy Spirit." Following lots of examination, it came down to the very fact that we were afraid of what might happen, and if we might lose the respect of our family and possibly the rejection of some of our friends. That did not seem to be a good enough reason to reject at least hearing the pastor out and seeing if what he was talking about was indeed true. I had taught for years not to let fear guide your heart in making decisions, so now I had to apply that same truth to my life in this situation as well.

So we called Pastor Bob and told him that we wanted to experience what he had. After all, he was a very godly man, and all of the elders in the church were embracing this, so we decided that we wanted to at least give it a try and see what might happen. Then, when Pastor Bob gently prayed for us, we simply and

The Royal Flush

profoundly received this new download from God regarding the Holy Spirit, and our lives began to change from that moment on.

The reality of the situation was that none of our family thought we were crazy, and I only lost one pastoral friend who to this day won't talk to me, but I gained thousands of others and am grateful to God for this new walk of spiritual provision in my life.

As I began to grow, learn, and experience this new realm of the Holy Spirit, I discovered that there was some new power that came with the offer and contract. I was not aware that I was lacking any power, but when I discovered what was available, I wondered why I had not been given this opportunity earlier in my walk with Jesus. Why had no previous pastor or college professor had ever shared this with me? Surely they knew about this power and the anointing and ability that came with it, so why were they hiding this information from me? I later learned why and will share it in a later chapter.

Diane and I were renting a nice townhouse in North Charleston, and if you know anything about Charleston, there are actually parts of it that are right at sea level (and in some cases below sea level). As a result, one of the problems we had in our area was that sand would filter into the underground water pipes of the city and then make its way into our home, lodging inside our pipes. We often took gritty showers from the sand in the water.

We had another problem, in that the sand would settle in the bottom of the toilet and cause our commodes not to flush properly. Frequently, we had to flush two to four times just to get the toilet to function properly. We had called the city numerous times about this, and city workers had come to our curb and cleaned out our pipes, but this was always and only a temporary fix. After a short period of time, the problems would surface again, with more sand clogging our pipes. It really was more than a nuisance.

So here I am at church, learning about the power of the Holy Spirit and seeing people receive prayer and being delivered from all sorts of things, so I had this idea that I should pray over my upstairs toilet in the townhouse, as that was where the scenario kept playing out. So I decided to be biblical about it, get some anointing oil, and go upstairs on a mission to see God work a miracle and fix my toilet.

I knelt down beside it and anointed the outside porcelain right near the handle, and I remember saying to God that if He could heal cancer, then surely He could also be a plumber and fix my toilet. After I laid my hands on that device, I simply asked God to do the rest and flushed the toilet. To my surprise, all of the water went down in a normal fashion, and from that day on it worked perfectly. We never had a problem with it again. Our showers were free from sandy debris, and our pipes were clean and clear.

What happened? Through faith and access to heavenly power, the Royal King of Heaven came to me in my time of need, visited my bathroom, and fixed our plumbing, thus giving us what I call the Royal Flush. Amen.

If you play poker or know anything about that card game, you are aware that a royal flush is the best possible winning hand you can have, consisting of an Ace, King, Queen, Jack, and 10, all of the same suit. The Kingdom of God is obviously not a card game, but with God in your life, you are assured of always having His very best for you every time. While the finger of God seems to be mostly for biblical events, and the arm of God reveals strength for nations, it is the hand of God that often rests on people, so one could say that you indeed have the most powerful hand available to you through the anointing of the Lord.

Now, fast-forward a couple of years. We were now at Faith Lutheran Church, a similar style church in the Houston, Texas, area, and I shared this same story in a message that I was

The Royal Flush

preaching. I later learned and heard the following testimony from a young lady named Cyndi.

Cyndi had some major car problems and anticipated car repairs, but she was without the financial ability to pay for these repairs. She took her car to one repair shop, and they estimated it would cost $1000. Then she took it to a second place, and that estimate was higher, near $1500, so she was discouraged and went home to think on the matter.

At her apartment, she suddenly remembered my "Royal Flush" testimony and decided that if God could fix a toilet, He could also fix a car. After all, how much harder could it be to have a God Who knows about plumbing and also knows about car mechanics? So she went out to the parking lot of her apartment complex and decided she wanted to anoint her car to be fixed. But when she got out there, she became nervous and slightly embarrassed, so she knelt down beside the side of the car near the tire, pretending to check the air pressure in one of the front tires, and prayed a simple prayer, asking God to fix her car. She then anointed the car with some cooking oil she had brought down from the kitchen.

A few days later, she had an appointment to take her car in to be fixed, hoping that they would work a financial deal with her so she could pay it over time, as she still did not have the money. After a short wait in the reception area, the shop manager came in with a kind of weird and puzzled look on his face, asking her why she brought the car back to them. She simply told them that they had given her the best financial bid to fix her car, and that is why she brought it to them.

But his next comment really startled her. He asked, "But why did you bring us a car that had already been repaired somewhere else?"

Now Cyndi was puzzled, and she asked, "What do you mean, somewhere else?"

And he said, "Well, the car is completely fixed, and there is nothing for us to do. Are you trying to make a joke here or make some kind of point?"

She apologized and said that she really thought the car was broken, and then she remembered her prayer in the parking lot a few days earlier and started jumping up and down right there in the car reception area. The shop manager thought she was nuts until she explained, and then he was okay with it. Cyndi later shared this testimony in church, and it was a blessing to many who knew her. This is an encouraging story because God still rewarded her even though she appeared to be ashamed to pray openly and also had little confidence after she had prayed. Even in our human weaknesses He is strong!

Revelation 19:10 says that the testimony of Jesus is the spirit of prophecy. I frequently encourage people not just to listen to a testimony and nod their heads in some sort of passive agreement indicating that they are genuinely glad for the person sharing the testimony, but also then to apply it directly to their lives in an active and even aggressive form of devotion. While doing this, they demonstrate that they trust God to similarly manifest for them in an area that they need as well. This is what Cyndi did, and it worked out well for her. And you can do it too.

These are called Kingdom Encounters. We have sincere faith that responds in a courageous way to something God did for someone else, and then we simply apply it and appropriate it for ourselves with an honest belief that God can and wants to do this for us too. There may be conditions and processes that God will initiate with us to get this accomplished, but that is okay because we have a good Heavenly "Dad" Who loves us, believes in us, and will work these things out in our lives for our good and for His good pleasure.

In John 1:14 this revelation is shared: "And the Word became flesh and dwelt among us, and we beheld His glory, the glory as of the only begotten of the Father, full of grace and truth." In verse seventeen, it is stated again in this way: "For the law was given through Moses, but grace and truth came through Jesus Christ."

Grace establishes us in a relationship with Jesus, with the hope and knowledge of eternal life after our time on earth, but truth is what gets the Kingdom moving while you remain on earth. There are many believers missing out on earthly Kingdom activity and ministry because they have never moved from grace to truth. Jesus was full of both. But it is sad to say that a rather large group of believing Christians remain satisfied to stay only in the grace realm and not venture out into an ongoing progressive truth pattern that will be enhanced and powered up by the presence of the Holy Spirit.

The Bible says that Jesus is the Way, the Truth, and the Life, and yes, there are people who want to know the life factor without walking in the way of truth. It is far easier to remain in a form of deception than to persevere into the truth, but it is only in the truth that you shall experience real freedom. Perhaps that is a description of you? Maybe, just maybe, you need additional truth revealed and implemented so that you can walk freely and without fear or hesitation in the life that Jesus wants for you. That possible deception will be addressed in chapter two.

In this book, I am going to share some things that hopefully will change your perspective about the Kingdom, and as that happens, hopefully that will translate into changing your actions too. Romans 12:1–2 speaks about a transformation of the mind that precipitates and necessitates future Kingdom action. So let's take a quick look at this passage right now:

> I beseech you therefore, brethren, by the mercies of God, that you present your bodies a living sacrifice, holy, acceptable to God, which is your reasonable

service. And do not be conformed to this world, but be transformed by the renewing of your mind, that you may prove what is that good and acceptable and perfect will of God.

This may be difficult to explain in writing. I know that you probably read the word *present* as in making a presentation, but I want you to think of the word in the terms of a Christmas present. Another way to say this is to use the word *present* as if it is happening right now in the present, not the future. Do you get it? So you make it your present in the present to present your body as a living sacrifice, holy and acceptable to God, which He then says is your reasonable service. In other words, God is not asking anything unreasonable of you. That aspect in and of itself is of great blessing and encouragement to all of us.

Then the Scripture goes on to instruct us to be transformed by the renewing of our minds. Our lives suffer from information overload, and in this age of technology and social media, they are only getting more and more clogged and congested with information. We must learn how to discern, distill and where necessary, delete that which is causing deliberate discord with the Kingdom of God.

Information is available in so many places and from so many sources, but true transformation is only available through the Word of God. So while I obviously encourage the reading of this book and others, make sure that you don't substitute books by human authors for the Word of God. If you do, you will get only glimpses of transformation with a lot of information. You simply must make reading God's Word a priority in your life. Paul instructed Timothy to give attention to the reading of the Word. And this came from the most educated apostle of that day.

Finally, Romans 12:2 concludes by noting that this all falls within the good, acceptable, and perfect will of God. What an amazing thing to know that you can walk in the perfect will of God and that you will be accepted! After grace has been appropriated and applied, God does not look at you or me and see us as being unacceptable. Rather, He sees someone good, who is being perfected, but He also sees someone who continually needs more truth.

Psalm 25:5 proclaims, "Lead me in your truth, and teach me for you are the God of my salvation." The Psalmist knew that we need to be led further into truth after our grace-filled salvation experience. This is further theophany beyond theology. In my book *Willing to Yield* I spent time discussing this instruction, and Jason also described this in his introduction to this book. To briefly review, theology is studying God's Word and theophany is experiencing God's presence. Both are necessary and essential in the life of a believer. Otherwise, what you end up with is a lot of puffed-up believers who know the Word of God but have not been transformed by it, resulting in a lack of His miraculous Kingdom presence and power. These people are professors, but not possessors. God can't bless what He doesn't possess.

Let's read this passage from Nehemiah 8, as it contains some amazing insights:

> Now all the people gathered together as one man in the open square that was in front of the Water Gate; and they told Ezra the scribe to bring the Book of the Law of Moses, which the LORD had commanded Israel. So Ezra the priest brought the Law before the assembly of men and women and all who could hear with understanding on the first day of the seventh month. Then he read from it in the open square that was in front of the Water Gate from morning until midday, before the men and women

and those who could understand; and the ears of all the people were attentive to the Book of the Law.

So Ezra the scribe stood on a platform of wood which they had made for the purpose; and beside him, at his right hand, stood Mattithiah, Shema, Anaiah, Urijah, Hilkiah, and Maaseiah; and at his left hand Pedaiah, Mishael, Malchijah, Hashum, Hashbadana, Zechariah, and Meshullam. And Ezra opened the book in the sight of all the people, for he was standing above all the people; and when he opened it, all the people stood up. And Ezra blessed the LORD, the great God.

Then all the people answered, "Amen, Amen!" while lifting up their hands. And they bowed their heads and worshiped the LORD with their faces to the ground.

Also Jeshua, Bani, Sherebiah, Jamin, Akkub, Shabbethai, Hodijah, Maaseiah, Kelita, Azariah, Jozabad, Hanan, Pelaiah, and the Levites, helped the people to understand the Law; and the people stood in their place. So they read distinctly from the book, in the Law of God; and they gave the sense, and helped them to understand the reading.

And Nehemiah, who was the governor, Ezra the priest and scribe, and the Levites who taught the people said to all the people, "This day is holy to the LORD your God; do not mourn nor weep." For

> all the people wept, when they heard the words of the Law.
>
> Then he said to them, "Go your way, eat the fat, drink the sweet, and send portions to those for whom nothing is prepared; for this day is holy to our Lord. Do not sorrow, for the joy of the LORD is your strength."
>
> So the Levites quieted all the people, saying, "Be still, for the day is holy; do not be grieved." And all the people went their way to eat and drink, to send portions and rejoice greatly, because they understood the words that were declared to them.

Think about it. The people stood for the reading of the Word of God and prostrated themselves before it, and it apparently transformed them. They recognized the higher power at work among them, and they responded with worship, honor, and declarations that were relevant, personal, and courageous as they worshipped the Lord in response to the reading of the Word. Had they only listened to the Word and nodded their heads in agreement, but not acted on it, there would have been no theophany or experience, which is often missing in many churches today.

I refer to these believers as "Cappuccino Christians" because oftentimes they loudly respond to how their coffee is to be experienced but quietly state that their faith should be a private matter. Where in the Bible are we told to keep quiet, not share our faith, and just have a private relationship with Jesus? Everything about Jesus speaks of sharing, witnessing, demonstrating the Kingdom, passing along hope to others, and displaying His power for the world to see. It's about touching the multitudes and developing disciples locally and abroad. You can't stay private and make disciples. That is hiding one's light under a bushel! So we must be captivated with His truth just like we are with His grace if we are going to become history makers and world changers. That is the call on our lives from the One Who created us. So His light must be shining full of energy, anointing and illuminating through us for others.

Years ago when living in Houston, we owned some property out in the country, and once a month or so, we would drive a pickup truck and haul our riding lawnmower out there, mow the fields, and clean up the area that we were cultivating for a future house. On one trip, we drove out and saw what appeared to be a small dead kitten in the road. Both my wife and I were saddened to see that little cat lying in the road. We worked on our property for roughly four hours and then headed home, driving by that kitten still lying in the road.

As our truck rumbled past that kitten I saw something move out of the corner of my eye that caught my attention. I immediately stopped the truck and backed up near the kitten. We discovered that this kitten was still alive! Who knows how long it had been lying in the road, but we knew it had been at least four hours. We scooped up the cat, put it in a bucket, and took it to our vet back in town. He was able to save the cat's life and find it a good home too. How in the world did that cat survive and not be totally squished on the road, and what made it raise its head just as I drove by?

Psalm 119:105 says that the Word of God is a lamp unto my feet and a light unto my path. Let me break this down just a little bit for you. The lamp unto your feet is like the reading lamp in your living room or den that gives just enough light for the immediate area, but the light on the path is like the floodlight in your backyard that shines and lights up the whole yard. There are times in your life and mine when God will give just a little light for

The Royal Flush

our immediate area, and at other times, He lights it all up gloriously so we can see the whole picture. He is always working at preserving our lives and rescuing us from destruction and death, just as we rescued that cat in the road.

Just yesterday, as I was reading a daily devotion that comes to my email, I discovered that it was about this very subject, so I want to share it with you. It was written by Kenneth Copeland, but I added a little bit to it too. I hope you enjoy it.

> In Him was Life and the Life was the Light of men. And the Light shines on in the darkness, for the darkness has never overpowered it. -John 1:4–5

> Whenever things around you get dark and you feel the devil is about to overpower you, remember this: You have the Light of the world in you, and try as they may, all the forces of hell can't put it out!

> Even when you're at your weakest, even when you feel like the light within you is small, the devil's darkness is no match for you.

> Let me show you what I mean. Imagine for a moment that you're in a large auditorium that has no windows or doors to let in outside light. The place is so black you can't see anything, not even your hand in front of your face. There's nothing around you but complete darkness!

> Now, imagine one little lightning bug flying around that auditorium. Every eye in there would turn toward it. As small as that little light is in

comparison to the great darkness around it, you would still be able to see it. That massive blackness wouldn't be able to do a thing to shut off that bug. Everywhere he flew, the darkness would just have to yield. It would always be dispelled by his light.

When the circumstances around you begin to get black and you're tempted to despair, think about that lightning bug. Meditate on the fact that Jesus Christ, the Light of the world, is in you. When the revelation of that hits you, you'll never again let the darkness back you into a corner. You'll start chasing it down—overcoming it with your light!

* * *

Jesus said for us to take His yoke, which is easy, and His burden, which is light. Yes, I know light there means "not heavy," but we can add value to taking the *light*, something that glows in the darkest room, and bring that light to ourselves as well as others when faced with surrounding darkness that is trying to overwhelm us. The speed of light travels very quickly, so when faced with any need, the speed of God's light can easily travel very quickly to you and your situation and bring light rays of hope and joy to your circumstances as God fills your room, your space, and your life.

In Psalm 32:7 we are told that God surrounds us with songs of deliverance. Listen for the songs. They are all around you. And these songs are full of

The Royal Flush

light! This little light of mine, I'm going to let it shine!

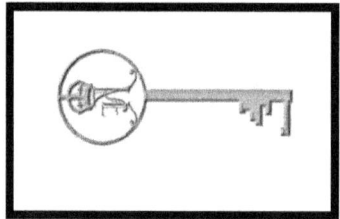

Kingdom Key #1: Walk in truth.

Psalm 119:30a encourages us to choose the way of truth. When first confronted with the Holy Spirit's power being offered by the pastor in Charleston, my response was to run or at least remain in an unreachable state. But over time, we decided to be open to what God might be revealing to us and to choose a path of truth. I am very glad we did. That decision has opened so many wonderful doors, and I am grateful to have experienced the theology and the theophany of that biblical experience.

Being filled and baptized by the Holy Spirit brought to my life a totally new expression of my faith and began a transformation process that is still going on to this day. It was and continues to be a good Kingdom Encounter.

Are there areas of your life where you feel the tug of God, but to this point you have been ignoring or resisting those tugs? What would it take to alter your course just a little bit and maybe trust the Lord with this new direction? How do you think you can respond differently to help bring and manifest the needed change that God desires for you in your life?

John 3:21 says it this way: "But he who does the truth comes to the light, that his deeds may be clearly seen, that they have been done in God." Are you ready to come to the truth that is in the light and the light that is in the truth? Don't be satisfied to stay in a dark environment with an occasional flickering blinking

The Royal Flush

light from one little lightening bug. Don't be like those in 2 Timothy 3:7 who are always learning but never come to the knowledge of the truth.

Ask the Lord to help you with this process. Be open to His leading. Be available to His plan. And take that first step toward His truth in this area of your life. You won't regret it. Just like the cat in the road, I believe God will pick you up, bandage you, and take care of you. Like the story of the Good Samaritan, God has a rescue plan ready to implement for you at the precise moment that you need it.

John 8:32 promises, "You shall know the truth and the truth shall set you free." Please remember the portrayal of God's Kingdom with the words in 3 John 4: "I have no greater joy than to hear that my children *are walking* in truth" (emphasis mine).

Today I might cite that a Royal Flush consists of the Father, Jesus, the Holy Spirit, the Word of God, and the Power of God, all wrapped up in grace and truth. That's part of the truth I walk in. How about you?

Chapter Two

The Tractor and the Rattlesnake

This is a story that makes my wife Diane cringe, but it fits the theme of this chapter, so I am going to share it. About thirty years ago when we lived in Texas, we had some friends who had a farm in another county outside of the Houston area. We would sometimes go out to help with projects and other various tasks. One time, I was invited to come and help bale hay. Since I grew up with citrus groves in California but had no experience with actual farming procedures and harvesting of products that did not grow on trees, I thought, *This should be fun*. I mean, how hard could it be?

So we set out to help. The bales were scattered all over the pasture, and several of us were assigned to different tractors that were pulling larger flat trailers. I soon found out that these bales of hay were not light. After doing this for the better part of the afternoon, I was growing tired in the Texas heat and began to carry the especially heavier bales up against my body near the belt line. That was a big mistake, for one of the bales was full of fire ants. I quickly had more bites than I cared for, but fortunately over the years I became immune to ant bites due to the sheer number of them that I had suffered.

Every time the trailer would get full, we would all jump on the trailer, sit on the bales, and ride back to the barn to unload the wagon. On one particular trip, I decided to ride standing on the hitch between the tractor and the wagon, balancing myself by holding onto the shoulders of the driver of the tractor.

Now this is where God intervened. You need to remember that I had no farming experience at all, so I did not know that riding in this particular position could actually be very dangerous if you don't know what you are doing. No one warned me of one particular impending and immediate danger.

You see, when the tractor turns, then the place where the wagon hitches onto the ball joint of the tractor also turns. I had my feet on a metal rod in a very narrow space. My feet were safe when the tractor was going straight, but had either of my feet remained in that place when the tractor turned, my right or left foot would have been crushed, and I most likely would have fallen under the trailer too, causing me great harm and pain. But for some reason, and it can only be God, I looked down on the first hard turn and saw what was about to happen and simply lifted my foot up when the metal of the trailer moved tightly against the ball joint. And at every turn, I either lifted my right foot or my left to accommodate this action that was taking place.

I learned something that day, and it changed my perspective, so I am using that story to launch this chapter. You see, the word *perspective* actually relates to the science of optics, specifically the science of vision and of seeing something in a different light. The word engages the thought of viewing objects that are in right relationships to other objects. The definition goes on to promote two phrases with two identical words, yet in opposite arrangement. They are *lookout* and *outlook*.

Lookout serves to express the idea of having a way of doing or seeing something with the idea of carefully watching with anticipation. And *outlook* is simply a way of thinking, dealing with an attitude or a point of view. Often your outlook will override your lookout, even though it is based on something you have not yet seen. The Bible calls this "faith" in Hebrews 11:1. This can be true in a positive or negative way. I see people move up to the altar area for prayer who are often in one of those two categories. They come believing and expecting to get well, while others come

The Tractor and the Rattlesnake

because someone dragged them there, and they feel compelled to do this, when in reality they don't believe anything miraculous could happen. They have different perspectives on why they are there and what might happen.

Let me illustrate this. I am guessing that if I was there in person with you right now and I asked you to tell me about some glorious sunrises or sunsets that you have seen in your lifetime, you could immediately jump into the conversation by sharing with me about the place where these spectacular events took place. And if it really made an impression, you might also have some pictures that you could show me and share to help me see what you enjoyed at that moment.

But the truth of the matter and the reality of the situation is that you and I have never seen a beautiful sunset or sunrise in our entire lives, because the sun does not set nor does it rise. The earth is revolving around the sun, so it only appears to us as if it is rising and setting. That is our perspective. In this case, our perspective is not really the truth or reality.

Years ago, when we lived in Dallas, I was driving home one evening, and it was nearly dusk, so you know that the amount of light is diminished at twilight time. I saw what looked like a very large rattlesnake in the culvert on the side of the road, and apparently a couple of other people saw it too. I quickly drove around the block and came to park my car a safe distance away from this snake. By now, several others were staring at it too. I got out of my car only to hear a warning from several people to stay back, as this was a very big snake. Every once in a while the snake would kind of rise up somehow. I thought that this was a kind of unusual move for a snake, but then I am no expert. As far as I was concerned, the only good snake was a dead snake.

I took another step toward the snake. One lady yelled at me to be careful, and she let me and everyone else know that she had called the animal control. It appeared to me that the snake once again moved in an upward fashion, but I noticed that this seemed to happen every time the wind would blow a little bit, which I thought was odd. And of course, it was continuing to grow darker by the minute, so if it became totally dark, we would all lose sight of this snake before the animal control folks arrived.

Just then, another wind gust came, and there went that snake up in the air again. I grabbed a flashlight from the car and took a few more steps toward the snake. At this point, I was now pretty close to it. Even though it was nearly dark and I was using only a small flashlight, in the very dim light of the evening, I could now see that this snake was in actuality only an old orange and gold flannel shirt that was rolled up in the gutter next to the culvert. Every time the wind would blow, it would kind of puff up like it was moving. I laughed to myself and decided to head back to the car and drive home before the animal control folks got there and embarrassed everyone.

What happened? Mine and many others' perspectives were obviously deceived, and part of the problem was that darkness was overshadowing our view, so our true vision of what the object was positioned all of us to be deceived.

Right in the middle of the word *perspective* is the root word for *spectacle*, or "spec." In the old days, people would refer to their glasses as specs. Perhaps in dealing with spiritual matters, we need to put our specs on and see things like God sees them rather than in our own distorted ways of viewing things. Do you see my point?

In the dictionary, one of the definitions of *deception* is that of an illusion. An illusion is a misleading appearance, or a false impression or perception, with a false idea, notion, or belief. Keep in mind that our enemy the devil comes to kill, rob, and destroy us, and he will attempt to use deceptions that are filled with illusions that cause us to take our eyes off Jesus and off the Word of God. His goal is to get us to look at this illusive distraction instead of what God is trying to reveal to us.

The Tractor and the Rattlesnake

Look at the warning in the Message Bible from Proverbs 14:18: "Foolish dreamers live in a world of illusion; wise realists plant their feet on the ground." And then an answer to this warning also in the Message Bible from Ecclesiastes 5:7: "But against all illusion and fantasy and empty talk there's always this rock foundation: Fear God!"

I believe I had an illusion that I would be safe on the back of the tractor, but God was gracious and kind to let me know of the potential danger and problems by having me look down just in time. There is no other explanation. It was a God viewpoint for sure, and He saved me from certain disaster.

He wants to do that for each of us on a daily and continuing basis, but we have to begin to have an outlook by looking out with Kingdom eyes, rather than with eyes that are only concerned about our own stuff, our own satisfaction, and our own benefit. God has great benefits that He wants to release in our lives, but we have to trust Him first above all else and through everything else.

Psalm 103:2 gives us this admonition: "Bless the Lord O my soul and forget not all of His benefits." The reason that every nation that previously knew God then fell away from His grace was because they forgot His testimonies and His benefits and went their own way instead. They took their eyes off God and onto all their own stuff. But God is looking for those whose eyes and perspectives are in tune with what He is doing, while remembering what He has done in the past too.

Second Chronicles 16:9 tells us, "The eyes of the Lord are looking to and fro throughout the whole earth, seeking to show Himself strong on behalf of those whose heart is loyal towards Him." God is looking for someone who is looking for Him. It's that simple.

My son Jason just posted on his weekly blog something pertinent to all of this, so I have cut and pasted part of an article that he wrote at college this week:[1]

I love a particular quote by John Bevere from his book *Driven by Eternity*,[2] which goes something like this: "For the believer, the question is not about *where* you will spend eternity. For the believer, the question is about *how* you will spend eternity." The same is true for this life on earth (which I believe is actually part of eternity). The question is not so much about *where* you will spend your life, but it is about *how* you will spend your life. We all are given the individual choices of how we will spend our time. It is up to us how we choose to spend that time. Show me how you spend your time, and I'll show you what's driving your life. [Let me (Jay) add, *Show me your checkbook and credit card receipts, and I will show you what's driving your life.*]

Is there a purpose behind what you're doing? Recently, I was reading a book by my friend Brandon Ryan entitled *The Emotional Struggle*.[3] In this book, Brandon includes a chapter dedicated to the importance of dreams—not dreams in the night, but dreams of purpose, vision, and planning for the future. He asks the readers what their dreams are. When I was reading that question, I really had to think hard to align my thoughts with the dreams in my life. What things was I doing that were aligned with the ultimate dreams God had given me? I had to think for a while to answer that question.

The reason is because I found myself caught up in doing so many things that it seemed more like I was randomly taking stabs in the dark, rather than purposefully aiming and shooting at a specific target. If I didn't step back and think about why I was doing what I was doing, I would have been in

The Tractor and the Rattlesnake

danger of losing sight of my purpose. The way I see it, humans have two choices—either to take stabs in the dark or to aim directly at the target.

Let me put it simply. To lose sight of your dreams is to lose sight of your purpose. To lose sight of your purpose is to lose meaning for life. To lose meaning for life is to go through the motions. And to go through the motions is to live a selfish life.

That's right. Going through the motions is selfishness. Some may think that pursuing their own dreams is selfish. But that's actually not true. Pursuing your dreams is actually quite selfless (that is, if you're pursuing the dreams God has given you). I'm not talking about self-promoting dreams for fame or fortune. I'm talking about true, legitimate dreams from God. In this case, the most selfless thing you can do is pursue the dreams God has given you. To not pursue those dreams is to selfishly hoard what God has given you, rather than releasing it to those who need to experience the benefits of that dream.

The dreams God has given you are to in some way expand the Kingdom of God. It may include things that you think pertain just to your life, but I have news for you: God is working with and on things with each of us that could usher in His presence at any moment and also bring His presence on the scene long after we have gone on to be with Jesus. It is about bringing His kingdom to earth today and then leaving that legacy for others to experience after us as well.

I recently read this quote on Facebook from my friend Jeni Langfeldt: "You only live once? False. You live every day. You only die once." Our perspective is that we only live once, but the reality is that, whether we accept and believe in Jesus or not, we will live forever. The better choice is to include Jesus so that you can live with Him forever, but either way, you will live forever. I am a spirit in a body, and while my body will die someday, my spirit will live on into eternity with Jesus, and I am hopeful that this is true for you too. My pastor, Jim Hart, would say it this way: "The me that you can't see is more me than the me that you see, because the me that you see isn't really me."

In Ephesians chapter two, we discover that while we were dead, Jesus made us alive. One of the main thrusts of this chapter is the revealing fact that life overtakes death, rather than the other way around, as some may think. Some people think that death overtakes life, but we know that light overtakes darkness, and in the same way life overtakes death. It may appear that when someone dies that death overtook them, but the reality is that death just showed up where the body was, but the spirit is still alive.

Jesus came that we might have an abundant life, and His life is consistently flowing into ours whenever and wherever we give Him that opportunity to do so. In the Old Testament, the people were given the opportunity to make a choice. God put life and death in front of them and told them to choose. And to this day, God will honor your choices. So I encourage you to make godly choices that He can infuse with His power and where He can deliver us from danger while we advance the Kingdom of God, as we focus our attention on Him. This will create new adventuresome Kingdom Encounters for you every day. God is a good God, and He not only loves us, but He *is* Love, and that love is permeating you right now as you read this book because you have made the choice to pursue His life.

God has an eternal perspective, while we often just have a short, earthly, "get by" perspective. We often view things as we see them, rather than how God sees them. So often when faced with a problem, we run to the phone instead of the throne.

The Tractor and the Rattlesnake

Frequently, when dealing with difficult situations, we spend more time talking to others than spending quality time sharing with the Lord. It is so easy to fall into this deceptive trap that entangles us with the problem rather than having an eternal perspective that looks up beyond the situation and past the weight of the difficulty to the One Who can easily solve and bring a resolution to the problem at hand. God knew there would be problems at hand, that is why it is often stated in the Gospels that the Kingdom of Heaven is at hand too.

The Bible says in Ephesians that I am seated with Christ in heavenly places right now. I have access to the same vision, the same outlook, and the same perspective as He does, and all I need to do is ask Him to show it to me. In John 16 we are told that God will show us things to come. I believe that because God says it, which is my theology to believe that. Then, I believe it because I have indeed seen the future before it happened, which is my theophany too. I get to experience God however He chooses to let me experience Him, and it is a great blessing for sure. God just loves to reveal His plans to His servants and share with them what is coming up so that they can prepare or avert such physical dangers as getting your foot crushed on a tractor.

What good earthly father and mother would let their child be intentionally hurt? Show me parents who would not yell at their own child if they sensed danger or saw it coming toward them? I believe that every parent would do what they could to prevent a tragedy from happening if they could, and our Heavenly Father loves us even more than our earthly parents do.

Let's read once again from the Message Bible in Colossians 3:1–2: "So if you're serious about living this new resurrection life with Christ, *act* like it. Pursue the things over which Christ presides. Don't shuffle along, eyes to the ground, absorbed with the things right in front of you. Look up, and be alert to what is going on around Christ—that's where the action is. See things from *his* perspective."

It's time to lift up our heads. It's time to stop being so self-absorbed. God working through you and me is the answer to many of the problems we see and experience around us. I love what Isaiah 60:1 shouts to us: "Arise, shine; for your light has come! And the glory of the Lord is risen upon you."

The word *arise* means to be revived, and *shine* means to be filled with bright fire. God wants us to reconnect and reestablish our first love in our lives. He desires for us to be up and moving, sharing the light in the truth like you read about in chapter one. His will is for the glory of the Lord to be rising upon us, not falling as some would pray or hope for. It is a great honor to represent Jesus in this realm, as described here in Isaiah.

So as I wrote about in chapter one, we walk in grace and truth, and now we are learning to walk in glory. A more accurate description might be to say that we walk in His presence. Getting and staying in His presence will change our perspective so fast it will amaze you. I know it has for me. There is nothing like being in His immediate and personal presence. Bill Johnson, in his book *Face to Face with God*, describes it this way: "When I married my wife, I wasn't interested in the concept or the theory of marriage. I wanted to experience marriage in all its privileges and responsibilities. People who respond to His presence properly can be trusted with increased favor."[4]

While praying for the sick in the past, I used to see what I would describe as hard cases, based on what I was seeing, but my perspective has changed so much that I really am not intimidated by any ailments, diseases, or injuries. I have prayed for and seen eyes and ears opened, people healed of cancer and leukemia, along with diabetes and Lyme disease. I have seen some lay down their walkers and others get out of wheelchairs and walk freely. My theophany caught up with my theology, and fear has been eclipsed and dispelled. The illusion and deception is gone in this area. Matthew 10:8 instructs us to heal the sick, so I am obeying that command. I know in Whom I believe, and I know that, according to the Book of Job, He is not only *my* redeemer and deliverer, but He is also available to be that Redeemer and Deliverer for *others* too. Yes, even you!

Now, I will be honest, I don't understand why everyone doesn't get well immediately, but I don't question it either, because there is enough evidence in the Bible that some were healed as they went. The ten lepers who were healed experienced that healing as they went, but we aren't told how far they actually walked. Maybe they went a block, but maybe they went a three-day journey. We aren't informed, but we do know that this manifestation happened later after they had been prayed for by the Lord. I just believe that Philippians 1:6 is true when it declares that we can be confident in God because He has definitely begun a good work in us, and He will indeed complete it. He is the One who always finishes and always finishes well.

Personally, I battled an incurable disease for three very long years, with pain being my number one symptom. I would literally wake myself up at night crying. My faithful and loving wife Diane would pray for me, and I would fall back asleep. There were many people praying for me in a church that believed in healing, and you can read more about this ordeal in my first book, *Downloads from Heaven*. The reality is that, while the doctors said I would never get well, someone forgot to tell that to Jesus, because He stepped in and healed me on June 1, 1991, and the symptoms with the pain never came back. Glory to God! I will never stop thanking God for this miracle and never forget to recall and remember His goodness and testimonies in my life. They propel me on when things are tough, and they help keep my personal perspective on track with what God is doing.

I choose to embrace what God is doing, rather than what He is not doing. Jesus said it best in John 5:19 when He responded that He only does what the Father is doing. Down in verse 30 of the same chapter, we read, "I can of Myself do nothing. As I hear, I judge and My judgment is righteous, because I do not seek My own will but the will of the Father who sent Me."

These verses and many others help keep my focus sharp and crystal clear. Otherwise, my own thoughts and actions will cloud what I am viewing. Then, the opportunity for distortion arises much more quickly, and the glory that is supposed to arise gets squashed by our concerns, worries, and fears.

In the past, I used to battle really intense headaches, and I discovered that using an electrical massager on my head and over my eyes could help eliminate the pain. But one day, I apparently used the massager too much and too close to my eyes, for it caused me to have an eye distortion to the point that for several weeks I had a cloudy image over my eye and could not see well with that eye at all. When reading, I had to use only my good eye, trying to keep the other one closed so as not to be distracted. This made many tasks very difficult, such as driving, computer work, writing, or any activity where anything other than casual eye contact was necessary. Through prayer, God healed it, as the eye specialists had no idea what to do or how to proceed and basically could offer me no hope at all. All we had was God.

As I am writing this, I am reminded of the passage in 2 Corinthians 7:5–6, which says, "For indeed, when we came to Macedonia, our bodies had no rest, but we were troubled on every side. Outside were conflicts, inside were fears. Nevertheless God, who comforts the downcast, comforted us by the coming of Titus."

I love this section! Don't you? Think about it. Paul had come to Macedonia, and he was basically dead dog tired. Every part of his body probably ached. His muscles were sore, and his ligaments hurt. Shoot, his hair, fingernails, and teeth probably were hurting too. And then there was trouble on every side. Not just the appearance of trouble, but actual trouble. No matter where Paul looked, there was trouble. He could slowly spin around and look in each direction and see trouble.

The Tractor and the Rattlesnake

On top of this, he tells us that on the outside were conflicts and on the inside were fears. Paul was not wimping out here or advising us to remain fearful, but rather just informing us of what was going on. Because he went on with the answer to the problem.

If he continued looking at all of these difficult situations, feeling all of these problematic issues, and hanging around all of these precarious circumstances, he knew that his perspective would be tarnished and ultimately ruined. He had to make a choice. And his choice was to trust the Lord through the efforts of a brother named Titus. What was he really doing? Keeping his perspective in line with the Word of God, anticipating that even in the midst of all these problems, he was going to have a Kingdom Encounter.

Can we learn from Paul's example? Can we apply that truth to our lives? Can we also anticipate having a Kingdom Encounter? I believe that simply raising my foot off the tractor hitch was an actual Kingdom Encounter.

Notice the phrase, "Nevertheless God." Would you say that out loud right now?! *Nevertheless God.* Say it again. *Nevertheless God.* Keep saying it until it is deep down in your spirit. Because it literally means to never settle for anything less than God. I want to be your Titus today and encourage you in this same pattern. Never settle for anything less than God. Never settle. Never! Never! Never settle.

I did not settle for the report of the water department in Charleston. Cyndi did not settle for her car repair estimate in Houston. And while it took three very long years, I did not settle for the report of the doctors who said I would never get well. As I write this today, I have a medical situation that only God can answer, and I am pressing in for my healing and deliverance from this affliction too.

You need to arise, shine, and let the glory begin to rise upon you right now. See yourself out of this mess, past the pain, beyond the relationship issue, and overcoming the problem.

Envision yourself as God sees you. Believe that life overtakes death and that light dispels darkness. Seek first the Kingdom of God and His righteousness, and watch how He then adds into you everything else that you have need of.

His glory is amazing! His provision is outstanding! His healing is life-changing! His love is unending! His truth is perfecting! His anointing is everlasting! His power is unleashing! His ability is creating! His joy is releasing! His vision is world-changing! His peace is assuring! His Kingdom is spreading! His child is developing! His favor is promoting! His hope is preserving! His faith is manifesting! His forgiveness is unending! His strength is attaining! And His presence . . . well, it's displaying and permeating.

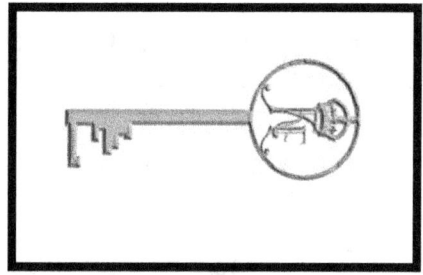

Kingdom Key #2: Change your outlook!

Your personal perspective is your passport to the Kingdom of God being revealed and manifested in your life. Either you believe He can and wants to use you to bring needed change within your sphere of influence, or you deny that option from ever happening, and you miss your opportunity to see something significant happen in your lifetime. Someone once wrote about the dash on a tombstone. A tombstone will often list a person's name and maybe some slogan that was important to them, but then there is a dash between the years, something like this: 1940–2012. What did you do (or what do you plan to do) with the dash that will someday appear between the dated years you were alive?

At the conclusion of Revelation 3:18, we are instructed to anoint our eyes with eye salve so that we might see. I believe God is driving home a prominent and critical point here in the last book of the Bible. The closer we get in time to the actual end times, the more we need to see with Kingdom eyes and have Kingdom understanding of what is happening around us.

Pay attention this week to what you watch and where you go. Look out for spiritual potholes and opportunities for your eyes to stray away from God's real purpose. Stay away from things that will cloud your vision, and ask God to help you with your official "dash" this week. Change your outlook to include ways to help change the spiritual climate and atmosphere around those whom you work with, live with, and fellowship with. Be attentive to the still, small voice of God this week, especially when warning you of personal danger. And be aware of deception and illusions that appear real but are just threats of the enemy to try to get you off track from God's purposes.

And if you find yourself on the back of a tractor, keep looking up, except when making a turn. That perspective may just save your life.

Chapter Three
Prison Break-In—Getting Cheesed

One of the philosophies of the Vineyard Movement is that God is breaking in all around us, and if we will just keep our eyes focused on the Lord and respond like Jesus did in John 5:19 where he replied that He only did what He saw His father doing, then we too will experience daily Kingdom encounters.

Years ago, I was on my way home from doing some prison ministry in Sugar Land, Texas. We had a program there called "one on one," and it was based on men on the outside who would commit to ministering to men on the inside of the prison. Both the men on the outside and on the inside made a commitment to meeting with their partner once a week for at least forty-three weeks a year. We would begin with a larger group time of worship, and then have about forty-five minutes of one on one time with our prison buddy. John Weesner, to whom this book is dedicated, later took over this ministry.

It was a particularly muggy evening as I drove home from prison ministry. I often like to drive with the windows down, and I was growing my hair longer in those days, so the wind would mess with it at times. I did and still have a receding hair line, and I would kiddingly remark that since I could not grow hair in the front, I would grow it in the back, so it was well over my collar. And I had worn older blue jeans and a t-shirt, as I had gone straight from doing some yard work to prison ministry that evening, so my clothes were kind of dirty and not up to the usual standard that the prison preferred for the visiting men.

There I was, driving with my hair in the wind. I decided to stop at a local Safeway store near our house to do some light shopping. I saw that there was working that evening a particular checkout lady named Judy. I had been witnessing to Judy over the past several months, so I was glad to see she was working, as I wanted to share some more with her.

So there I was, this 6-foot, 7-inch tall guy with longer hair tousled by the wind, wearing older and slightly dirty clothes. As I approached Judy with my items on the conveyor belt to be scanned, she greeted me with a big smile and asked, "How are you this evening?" Out of my mouth came these words: "Fine, for a guy who just got out of prison."

At this point, a number of people behind me made some groaning noises and small talk in reply to that comment of mine. But I soon clarified, sharing how we would go into the prison every Tuesday evening to minister to the inmates, and that seemed to put everyone at ease. Judy listened as she rang up my groceries, and then at one point I simply asked her if she would like to make a commitment to Jesus that night with a time of prayer.

I was sincerely hoping she would say yes, and felt like if she did, I could wait for her to get through with these customers and then find a quiet place in the store to have this prayer. But she surprised me by blurting out, "Yes, and let's do it right here and right now!"

Wow, that was a shock, for sure. So I simply said, "Let's pray." And—I am not kidding here or exaggerating—all the people waiting in the aisle behind me bowed their heads in prayer too. I had a nice prayer with Judy right there in the checkout line at Safeway. It was very cool. That night, Judy was freed from the prison of sin and led to a personal encounter with Christ.

As I continue with some more thoughts from the previous chapter on changing our perspective, let me bring in a verse from Psalm 102:13: "You will arise and have mercy on Zion. The time

Prison Break-In—Getting Cheesed

to favor her has come, yes the set time has come." Let me say up front that I am not into predestination at all, but rather I understand it with the eyes that see like God does in that He sees things in the future, and in that foreknowledge, He then sometimes uses the word *predestination*. One such use of this word can be found in Ephesians 1:7–13:

> In Him we have redemption through His blood, the forgiveness of sins, according to the riches of His grace which He made to abound toward us in all wisdom and prudence, having made known to us the mystery of His will, according to His good pleasure which He purposed in Himself, that in the dispensation of the fullness of the times He might gather together in one all things in Christ, both which are in heaven and which are on earth—in Him. In Him also we have obtained an inheritance, being predestined according to the purpose of Him who works all things according to the counsel of His will, that we who first trusted in Christ should be to the praise of His glory.
>
> In Him you also trusted, after you heard the word of truth, the gospel of your salvation; in whom also, having believed, you were sealed with the Holy Spirit of promise, who is the guarantee of our inheritance until the redemption of the purchased possession, to the praise of His glory.

God's foreknowledge joined with our faith brings tensional truths together such as predestination and election. Also, with words like "set time," there could be some confusion on our part regarding what God is trying to convey. The set time is really a time to signal something. God is arising on your behalf, often working behind the scenes setting things up so that when you respond in obedience and faith, then the set time of favor literally drops into your lap because of your faithfulness and His.

In chapter two, I briefly shared with you from Isaiah 60:1, about what happens as we arise and shine. That shining is really just letting God be God in every circumstance and area of life. Then, when others look at us, regardless of our situation or circumstance, they are drawn to the light of God in us. As God then sees us responding in faith and being faithful with the assigned task, He too has a set time to bless, encourage, heal, and provide in whatever fashion or response is merited by His kids walking in obedience, faith, and love. This creates another tensional truth of yielding with an encounter that Jason wrote about in the introduction.

In the natural there is a set time for most of us to get up, eat, get paid, watch certain TV shows or sporting events, go to church, have business appointments, enjoy fellowship with friends, get the kids to school, go to the dentist, and so on and so on. We have calendars, text reminders, phone alarms, and all sorts of electronic forms of reminders to keep us on track and on time with the many appointments that we all experience in our busy world.

But God is also looking for a set time to break in and use you and me to set the prisoners free. He is an opportunistic Father who loves to intervene at just the right moment, bringing needed relief, comfort, and sustaining power, supernatural presence and sudden provision to ultimately change a situation and make everything better. It's His nature to love us this way. He enjoys it, and as we saw in a previous chapter, is looking for those whom He can show himself strong to (2 Chronicles 16:9).

In Hebrew, the words *set time* simply mean signal. I am not a biblical language scholar but I do know a little Greek and a little Hebrew. The Greek owns a restaurant and the Hebrew owns a

Prison Break-In—Getting Cheesed

supermarket (smile). In the introduction, Jason also referred to set times as God's *kairos* moments, which are indeed Kingdom encounters. These *kairos* moments signal to us that God is encountering us with His Kingdom in a deep and powerful way.

God uses signals to get our attention. Here in Nebraska where I currently live, there are signal lights on many highways, and in advance of those lights are warning yellow lights that begin to blink, letting you know that the signal light is about to turn from green to yellow. These warning lights are set at a certain distance so that if you see them flash even just as you are passing them, you will not be able to speed up fast enough to make the green light. Thus, most folks understand the need for gradual braking so they can be prepared as that light turns from green to yellow and then red. If, on the other hand, you are indeed past these warning lights when they begin to flash, and you are maintaining the current speed limit, you should have enough time to make it past the green light before it changes to yellow. These warning lights blink at the precise set time to alert drivers of this needed reduction in speed to avoid accidents and follow the rules of the road.

As I was checking out of Safeway, a set time happened. God was breaking into Judy's life that very evening, and everything was set for a party to begin happening in heaven. All that was needed was for me to follow the instructions of the Lord and stay on track with what He was doing. So I say again, I work hard at positioning myself to embrace what God is doing, not what He is not doing. If Judy had not been ready that night I would not have pushed her to some point of despair and anguish, but God knew that the fruit was ripe.

Let me illustrate. I grew up in Southern California, and we had a variety of citrus trees and other fruit trees on our property. Orange trees were my favorite fruit trees, partly because orange is my favorite color, but also because I just loved eating oranges. We often would work in the yard, and when tired or thirsty, just pick a juicy orange, eat it, and then return to our task. In California we generally got two crops a year, and with the variety of fruit trees we had, we were almost certain to have some kind of citrus fruit ready to eat year round.

When an orange tree first bursts into bloom with glorious orange blossoms, the aroma is heavenly. Then, the blossoms begin to germinate into tiny, hard, green balls that grow into larger, hard, green balls, ultimately turning into slightly softer, larger, orange balls, giving the appearance that they are ripe.

However, an orange tree can fool you, in that while the color looks correct, the ripening process has not yet fully matured. For you see, if you try to pick an orange before it is ripe, you will most likely tug on the branch and pull the branch off the tree with you. But when the fruit is ripe, the slightest and gentlest touch, with just a tap of your finger, will cause that orange to drop right into your hand. When that happens, you know you have arrived at the set time of harvest for this amazing citrus fruit we simply call an orange.

The set time had come for Judy that evening. God's gentle wind was blowing, and the fruit of the Spirit of love fell from heaven, with just a slight nudge or a tap from God's finger, and landed squarely in Judy's heart. She was forever changed.

Before I go on, maybe this pertains to you right now. Maybe the set time has come, and it is time to allow God to release the fruit of the Spirit that you need in your life right now. They are listed below for you to read and absorb.

Galatians 5:22–23 says, " But the fruit of the Spirit is love, joy, peace, longsuffering, kindness, goodness, faithfulness, gentleness, self-control. Against such there is no law." Let's take a moment to pause, pray, and ask God to pick His fruit that we need in our lives. Ask Him to deliver that fruit to you in response to your prayer. Will you do that? Pause and Pray. Tap the Fruit. Pause . . . pray!

Prison Break-In—Getting Cheesed

Okay, at this point I want to share some more prison news with you. At Eagle's Nest Worship Center, the church we attend in Omaha, we pray for several men who are incarcerated at prisons in Nebraska and in a couple of other states as well. One of them is a guy named Aaron, who has launched a ministry from inside the prison walls in which inmates take the money that they earn (normally one dollar a day) and spend that on honey buns, toothpaste, and other necessities. They hand these items out in the yard and offer to talk to the other inmates and pray with them. The prayer requests are then sent to our church every month, and our pastor, Jim Hart, dedicates time in the service to read these notes and distribute the prayer requests to the members, who then take them home and pray over them. We actually have seen some men released early who now are attending our church and have glowing testimonies.

So I am going to submit to you one such letter from Aaron. I know him personally, having visited him in prison a few times at Tecumseh State Prison in Nebraska.

> What is up with this God we serve? I mean seriously, can anyone tell me why He does things so big? When He wants to prove a point, it's not with an appropriate hand; it's with an abundant stroke of power. A parted Red Sea, the belly of a whale, 5000 people full of a couple of fish, or a risen Christ; those are the signs He sends to get our attention. This month's lesson for me is divine appointments *[perhaps set times]*.
>
> It was enough for me when I was transferred here to Omaha Correctional Center from Tecumseh. I was like, "Okay, I gotcha Lord. Message received." But God wasn't done. My cellmate offers to move out,

61

and my Christian brother, Steve, moves in. So now it's two Tecumseh brothers in a cell, and I'm like, "Really, Lord, I'm with you! Stop blessing me! But of course, He wasn't done yet, and as we went out this morning for Operation Another Option, He continued to drive home His point.

Normally, we go out in the afternoon so that we can be in church in the morning, but this morning we felt led to go out and miss church. So we go out, and it's like divine appointment after divine appointment.

We walk in on two guys playing dominoes, and one of them says, "My mom was just telling me about this. She goes to Eagle's Nest." I asked him his name, and I'm like "Dude! My Mom told me to be on the lookout for you because your Mom spoke to her." I tell him about Jesus and how this moment was divinely appointed for us to meet. We spoke for a few minutes and really bonded in Christ.

We get up from the table, go to the next, and there is man by himself writing a letter. Steve gives him the business, and after the man says, "I'm an agnostic, but this week I have been talking to God and asking Him to do something in my life as proof." I nearly shouted, "Here it is!" I spoke to him about how God heard him speak and sent Steve and me over to talk to him. We had a great conversation after that, and I believe God is going to keep revealing himself to that man.

Prison Break-In—Getting Cheesed

Next, we get up, and a guy is walking toward us. We stop and speak to him, and he tells us he is mad at God right now because he has lost all of his family during his 15 years inside, and now he has none to get out to see. Steve starts to minister to him, telling him about Job losing his family but how God can replace what we've lost. I told him how I was once shaking my fist at God because of the loss of a best friend, and how I wasted eight years of my life doing it. I told him if he unclenched his fist of fury and raised his hands in worship, that God would do things in his life. As we were talking to him, you could physically see tension leaving his body. He told us how he was a believer, and he really needed to talk to us this morning. We parted ways, with plans to kick it later.

We continued to pass out stuff and share the Gospel, and we kept on running into people who were divinely appointed to meet this morning. We finished with two guys. We only had two gifts left, and there were four guys walking toward us, so we let God lead us to them. We gave them the "spiel," and as we were speaking, smiles slowly creased from their faces until they were full-out cheesing at us. When we got done, they couldn't wait to tell us how they were just talking about what we just told them.

[Just so you know, according to World Wide Words: Investigating the English Language across the Globe, *"The exclamation* cheese!, *often written* jeez!, *is definitely a euphemism for* Jesus!*"]*[5]

We spoke for about five minutes about prayer, faith, baby-momma drama, and overcoming hate with love. When we parted ways, we were blown away by our happenstance meeting. I have a feeling that this place is just waiting to explode for Christ. God is up to something here. I have this itching feeling in my spirit that there are men on the verge of surrender—men waiting on the prodding of God to make a commitment. I can't wait!

Divine appointments. There are no coincidences. There are no "lucky moments." There are only opportunities to step out into the moments God has appointed for us. This is lesson 101 in what has been my spiritual education here in prison. Thank you, Jesus.

One of my favorite prison break-in and break-out stories is found in Acts 12:5–17 when Peter was in prison. Here is the account for you to consider:

> Peter was therefore kept in prison, but constant prayer was offered to God for him by the church. And when Herod was about to bring him out, that night Peter was sleeping, bound with two chains between two soldiers; and the guards before the door were keeping the prison. Now behold, an angel of the Lord stood by him, and a light shone in the prison; and he struck Peter on the side and raised him up, saying, "Arise quickly!" And his chains fell off his hands. Then the angel said to him, "Gird yourself and tie on your sandals"; and so he did. And he said to him, "Put on your garment and

Prison Break-In—Getting Cheesed

follow me." So he went out and followed him, and did not know that what was done by the angel was real, but thought he was seeing a vision. When they were past the first and the second guard posts, they came to the iron gate that leads to the city, which opened to them of its own accord; and they went out and went down one street, and immediately the angel departed from him.

And when Peter had come to himself, he said, "Now I know for certain that the Lord has sent His angel, and has delivered me from the hand of Herod and from all the expectation of the Jewish people."

So, when he had considered this, he came to the house of Mary, the mother of John whose surname was Mark, where many were gathered together praying. And as Peter knocked at the door of the gate, a girl named Rhoda came to answer. When she recognized Peter's voice, because of her gladness she did not open the gate, but ran in and announced that Peter stood before the gate. But they said to her, "You are beside yourself!" Yet she kept insisting that it was so. So they said, "It is his angel."

Now Peter continued knocking; and when they opened the door and saw him, they were astonished. But motioning to them with his hand to keep silent, he declared to them how the Lord had brought him out of the prison. And he said, "Go, tell these things to James and to the brethren." And he departed and went to another place.

Let some of these thoughts (cerebrations) break into your cogitation, deliberation, reflection, intellection, contemplation, speculation, and meditation while pondering rumination. The church was praying for Peter's release, but not expecting it, because when the people heard that Peter was actually outside of the prayer room or house church, they thought that Rhoda was imagining this. In reality, Peter had more trouble getting into the prayer meeting than he did getting out of prison.

Notice too, that the angel did his part, and Peter did what he could do too. Peter had to get up, get dressed, put on his sandals and actually follow the angel. I often say that we do the possible and God does the impossible. We should do the natural and God will do the supernatural. In fact, God's natural is the supernatural. So we should do the possible and ask God to do the impossible. Yes, it is possible that I said that twice but in two different ways, but I am trying to drive home this impossible possible point, and that is that God loves to do these kinds of impossible things for His kids.

In Luke 1:37, we are told that with God nothing is impossible. Now, we understand "nothing" to mean not anything or "no thing." We could also say that it is a thing that does not exist. But God does exist, so having something that does not exist is impossible.

Remember creation; it did not exist, but with God, that was impossible, so it came into existence. With God, having nothing, seeing nothing, doing nothing, and actually nothing in and of itself existing through nonexistence is impossible with God.

With God, nothing is not the opposite of something, implying that with something, there is indeed something, but if nothing is the opposite, then there would be no thing, and with God that is impossible. You better read that one again. You better read that one again. You are not seeing double. You really should read that one again.

Prison Break-In—Getting Cheesed

Here's another way to think about it: There are things that are going to be created in the next five years that don't exist now, except with God, they do, because He is the Alpha and Omega, the Beginning and the End. While He is here with us, He is also there five years from now, so what appears not to exist for us already exists for Him, which is why nothing is impossible. God simply reveals it at the precise moment. It's already been created.

That's why Romans 4:17 is just as real and alive and in our lives today as it was when it was written: "(As it is written, "I have made you a father of many nations") in the presence of Him whom he believed—God, who gives life to the dead and calls those things which do not exist as though they did."

According to Wikipedia, the etymology of *exist* has this description: "The word 'existence' comes from the Latin word *existere* meaning 'to appear', 'to arise', 'to become', or 'to be', but literally, it means 'to stand out' (*ex-* being the Latin prefix for 'out' added to the Latin verb *stare*, meaning 'to stand')."[6] So, existence is arising out of nothing literally to stand out and appear. That is why Isaiah 60:1 is a reality too, because the glory of God, rather than descending down from Him, arises out of us as people who are seemingly nothing compared to God. We walk in faith and respond with trust, and the glory of God appears on us from within us. You might have to read this whole paragraph again as well.

Our response to God for things that exist is offered to us in Revelation 4:11: "You are worthy, O Lord, to receive glory and honor and power; For You created all things, and by Your will they exist and were created."

Don't let today's limitations place your mind in prison, thinking that there is no other alternative or option. When people are in prison, someone else holds the key, and the prisoners can only come and go when the guard allows them to. This prison aspect will be discussed in a later chapter dealing specifically with captivity. You have God's key to unlock His treasures.

Here are some possible prison examples. By agreeing with a medical professional who gives you no hope, you then reduce your situation to nothing, but nothing is impossible with God. The doctor may give you no hope, but the report of the Lord is that while the doctor can do nothing, God can't do nothing because nothing is impossible, so an answer is possible and through faith is accessible to you right now. The same is true of the marriage counselor who urges divorce, stating that there is nothing more either of you can do. But nothing is not an option with God, and there is plenty more that He can do. Your financial accountant may sit you down and say that you have done everything possible and that there is nothing more that can be done to fix this problem. But God, Who is the God of impossibilities, can indeed make a coin appear in a fish's mouth, feed thousands of people with small amounts of food, and bring in so large of a catch of fish that the nets begin breaking, even though others may have shared that it is impossible. God's keys unlock God's treasures, and He offers the keys of the Kingdom to us.

Someone once said that God is nowhere. But if you simply divide that word between the *w* and the *h* you have, "God is now here." It is just a matter of our perspective. Don't listen to others who don't have a Kingdom perspective; listen to God. Others with only a worldly viewpoint will often give you *no* hope, but simply by adding a *w* (which is the initial letter of the supernatural Word of God) to the end of the natural word *no*, we learn that God will give us *now* hope, based on His Word, which says nothing is impossible.

Exodus 34:10 gives us this insight: "And God said, 'As of right now, I'm making a covenant with you: In full sight of your people I will work wonders that have never been created in all the Earth, in any nation.'" And since nothing is impossible, we can count on this kind of ongoing creation to continue as the world needs new revelation and new substance to support that revelation.

Prison Break-In—Getting Cheesed

I believe prayer is the launching pad for ever-increasing revelation. Larry Lea used to teach that intercession brings revelation, and revelation then brings manifestation. I added that manifestation brings exaltation, which returns us to more intercession. We see from this perspective that our lookout and outlook are affected by prayer or intercession, bringing us to a deeper level of revelation. This revelation then adds the substance of manifestation. And faith is the substance that brings manifested evidence on the scene.

The manifestation can either be miraculous or something physical and tangible. Obviously, if it is coming directly from God, we could label it all as miraculous, but I am trying to make the distinction here between supernatural provision, such as hearing loss restored or back pain disappearing, versus a new product design or something technological that enhances our lives in an ongoing way. So, like Peter, we do the natural and God does the supernatural. We pray and intercede, and God brings the revelation, coupled with the manifestation, to solve the problem. That revelation may come at just the right moment. Check out the illustration below to substantiate my point.

In chapter five, "Being Uncommon," in my book, *Willing to Yield*, I recalled a time when I was exiting from the dentist's office after a rather lengthy procedure. In my head, I was going over the itemized bill, I started complaining in my mind about the expense, and then I remembered some other bills at home and some items that needed repair. This simply began a downward spiral of mental complaining and really whining too. But before I reached my car, God interrupted my thoughts and asked me if I was blessed. I paused a moment, and I responded, "Yes, I am blessed."

Then God questioned me further, "So what's the problem?" That comment in the form of a personal question changed my perspective for the rest of the day and even the week. I had received an encounter from God, a divine appointment, and definitely a *set time* moment. God had intervened, spoken to me, transformed my thought life with two questions, and imparted something to me that I remember to this day. It's been said that God may be able to turn the water into wine, but He can't turn your whining into anything.

Leonard Ravenhill wrote in his book *Revival God's Way*, "The opportunity of a lifetime must be seized within the lifetime of the opportunity." There are opportunities set in front of us daily. We have the choice whether to walk through them or not. If it was simply a matter of predestination, then there would be no choice in the matter, and everything that God planned would happen. But we know that we have all missed opportunities that God set before us.

Someone once said, "Though no one can go back and make a brand new start, anyone can start from now and make a brand new beginning." That is the hope of every released prisoner. The Bible has many prison stories, from Joseph in the Old Testament to Paul and Silas and Peter in the New Testament, where God intervened and broke into a prison to help those imprisoned break out of prison so that others could experience God breaking into their lives with opportunity after opportunity.

What Ravenhill is saying is that sometimes these opportunities have very narrow windows of time and space allotted to the circumstances associated with them. Because of that, the need to stay focused on what God is doing is critical in the life of a believer in Jesus.

Of course we have the choice and the freedom to turn God down when He prompts us in a certain direction. Galatians 5:13 offers this advice: "For you, brethren, have been called to liberty; only do not use liberty as an opportunity for the flesh, but through love serve one another." Paul writes here in Galatians that many of these opportunities are presented to us to serve one another. That is exactly what the above prison letter was about.

Prison Break-In—Getting Cheesed

Galatians 6:10 carries this message another step or two by adding in all men, especially the household of faith: "As you have the opportunity, do good unto all men, especially the household of faith." It's as if God is saying, "Look for opportunities. Look for ways to bless and encourage. Seek out strategies to carry out this plan of God's that in turn may well open up Kingdom Encounters that would not have otherwise been possible had you not been willing. Acts 10:38 shares with us how even Jesus was anointed to do good. We often miss this point, aiming instead at the supernatural stuff, but often simply doing good opens up great avenues for us to encourage others to have Kingdom encounters with Jesus today.

That's one reason I am a proponent of Servant Evangelism, made quite popular by Steve Sjogren, formerly the senior pastor of the Cincinnati Vineyard, a megachurch in that region. You can learn substantially more about Servant Evangelism at *www.servantevangelism.com*, which I highly recommend. This simple yet kind and easy approach to evangelism has an element of serving to it that takes many in our society today completely by surprise. The process emphasizes godly principles, coupled with sheer energy and prayer to make a huge difference in the lives of others, while giving people an opportunity to encounter Jesus. I could tell you some great stories, but for now, I will simply suggest you read the website.

As I proceeded out of the dentist's office, God was breaking into my thought life, adding new Kingdom viewpoints that changed my outlook, which in turn altered my lookout. Combined with this chapter on Kingdom Encounters, God left me with this opportunity to "cheese" others that day and then also you today as you read this chapter.

The Kingdom of God is breaking in right now. It's a prison break, but one that is designed to set the captives free and bring new life to those who have been bound up from previous encounters with the enemy who came simply to kill you, rob from you, and destroy your life. Jesus does not want that to happen, and neither do I. Let's look at the next Kingdom Key to begin the process to unlock your prison door, whatever it may be.

Prison Break-In—Getting Cheesed

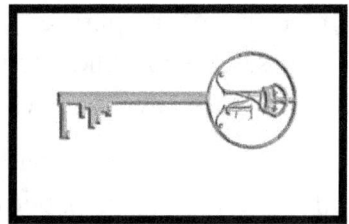

Kingdom Key # 3: God has a "free" get out of jail card.

In the game of Monopoly there is a "Get Out of Jail Free" card that enables you to continue the game if you should land in jail. God has something similar, and it is contained within the anointing of believers.

Luke 4:16–19 shares this wonderful account:

> So He came to Nazareth, where He had been brought up. And as His custom was, He went into the synagogue on the Sabbath day, and stood up to read. And He was handed the book of the prophet Isaiah. And when He had opened the book, He found the place where it was written: "The Spirit of the LORD is upon Me, Because He has anointed Me, To preach the gospel to the poor; He has sent Me to heal the brokenhearted, to proclaim liberty to the captives, and recovery of sight to the blind, to set at liberty those who are oppressed; to proclaim the acceptable year of the LORD."

That phrase, "to proclaim liberty to the captives," is an announcement of freedom to prisoners who are bound up in personal prisons of mental, emotional, and spiritual proportion from which it appears there is no way of escape. However, let me remind you of the phrase "nevertheless God." God is in the saving business. He knows how to set captives free. He holds the keys and releases those keys to us when we need them.

You may think that you are bound up, and held in prison with a habit or a sin pattern, but God has a way out. His word is sure, and His methods are proven. Your opportunity to escape and never return is possible if you respond to His ways and means of getting this accomplished. And if you think you can get out on your own without God, then just look around you now and wonder why that hasn't happened to this point.

Jesus was quoted as saying, "Whom the son sets free is free indeed." So this is your opportunity. Because the best start to Kingdom life is to walk out of your own bondage as a free person in Jesus Christ. Approach God right now in prayer, and lay it out in front of Him. Don't beat around the bush. Just tell Him what imprisons you and keeps you from having consistent Kingdom Encounters. And repent of any sins associated with these actions. His forgiveness is also a pardon, and He can and will set you free if you are willing. What is your verdict? The anointed pardon is sitting on His desk, but it needs your signature of agreement.

In this case, He has already done the supernatural and is just waiting for you to do the natural. Your "nothing" becomes His "something" through His impossible verdict. You are Free! Now, practice Galatians 5:1: "Stand fast therefore in the liberty by which Christ has made you free, and do not be entangled again with a yoke of bondage."

More on bondage and captivity will be discussed in a later chapter.

Chapter Four
Anointed Afterglow

Many find it is interesting that Paul's letters to the various churches in the New Testament, such as to the Ephesians, Philippians, Colossians, Galatians, and Romans, were just church newsletters at the time but now are the anointed Word of God. What are the amazing possibilities of some of the routine things you are doing today that may be history-making events in the future? Don't think of anything in the Kingdom as being insignificant. All have value, all have influence, and all have the ability to produce mighty exploits for God.

It is important that we maintain and continue to practice these two verses: Galatians 6:10, which states, "Therefore as we have the opportunity, let us do good unto all men, especially the household of faith"; and Acts 10:38, which reads, "How God anointed Jesus of Nazareth with the Holy Spirit and with power, who went about doing good, and healing all who were oppressed by the devil, for God was with Him."

In the Galatians passage we are instructed to do good, especially as it relates to those within the household of God, or of those with likeminded faith. And in Acts, we often focus on the anointing to participate in and do the supernatural, missing the little ingredient of doing good. That aspect of doing good, helping others, and doing the natural kind of stuff, is also very important. In fact, it really is critical in the development of our faith and the precision formatting of how God is molding us for future Kingdom ministry. There are many people who have a supernatural anointing for signs and wonders and things that make you respond with *oohs* and *ahhhhs*, but then they don't have the track record of good intentions followed with good advice and good habits that flow into good works. The integrity issue opens up things that then make us respond with *ohhhh*!

Ephesians 2:10 declares this: "For we are His workmanship, created in Christ Jesus for good works, which God prepared beforehand that should walk in them." This aspect of doing good and being His workmanship is part of His master plan. We literally are a piece of work, or a piece of the work that needs to be added to other pieces to complete the Kingdom process and promote the Kingdom Encounter.

After the famous section of Ephesians 4:11 that many often refer to as the five-fold ministry, we then come to verse 16 which commissions us to act in this manner: "From whom the whole body, joined and knit together by what every joint supplies, according to the effective working by which every part does its share, causes growth of the body for the edifying of itself in love." Each of us is working together, which then causes growth. And we do so using our own strengths, gifts, and callings.

First Peter 4:10 encourages us with these words: "As each of you has received a gift minister it as good stewards of the manifold grace of God." We are to steward our gifts, and use them for God's glory. It's not about us, and it's not about how good we look or how much anointing we have, but rather it is about promoting the Kingdom in a way that literally points others toward Jesus. This truly is a challenge because so many either don't know what their gifts are, or they don't like them and want something else that seems to be more fitting to their line of thinking, especially when it comes to Kingdom activity and action.

However, 1 Corinthians 4:2 challenges us that the requirement of stewards is faithfulness. We are to be faithful with what God gives us and release those gifts to build up the body and encourage others, while walking in humility and grace to serve others and Jesus. It really is pretty simple.

Let me illustrate this with something I call the Jeremiah Project. Several years ago, a pastor friend named Jeremiah who lives in the area called me up and asked me to come over and meet with him and his wife at his home. They began to share with me a number of things that were breaking down in their home and some of the distress points that they were living in at the time. There were carpet squares on top of holes in the rugs, cracked window panes, ceiling fans with one or no paddles, and cupboards in the kitchen hanging by one hinge. Plus, you would often get shocked when touching almost every light switch in the house.

He and his wife were sleeping in the cold basement that literally had only one heating vent, as they were allowing their children to be upstairs in the warmer rooms. There were so many things wrong that I was a bit overwhelmed but also honored that they would ask me to help and assist them. As they were sharing, I thought that perhaps I could maybe raise $5,000 to help with some of the more immediate needs.

So I put the matter to prayer and began to get a plan that I believe was from the Lord. Keep in mind, I am not a contractor and know nothing about plumbing, electrical, sheetrock, carpentry, or any other craftsman's trade to help in this kind of situation. My only forte would be that of landscaping, as I do it as a hobby and have had our house displayed in local garden shows and been chosen as yard of the month. But you definitely do not want me working on your house in any way, shape, or fashion.

God has given me the ability to network, so I launched out in that realm. I discovered a contractor who wanted to do some of the volunteer work for Pastor Jeremiah and his family. This, in turn, led me to contact a few friends and some local churches to begin the process of helping this family. What ensued was nothing short of a miracle, as the churches (or should I say, the church in Omaha) came together to seize the opportunity in an incredibly marvelous way. This can only be described as a God-given encounter that began to fulfill Galatians 6:10, which again says,

"Therefore, as you have the opportunity, do good unto all men, especially the household of faith."

Over the next eight months, various supplies and resources were donated through churches and Christian business leaders who somehow heard about the project. Many times, people would contact me without any knowledge of what was needed and offered exactly what we required that week to complete a project, whether that be the precise funds for the work, or the materials on our wish list to complete a task.

Now, here are some of the projects that were completed: new double pane windows for the entire house; new solid core exterior doors with deadbolt locks; new carpet for the entire house; and new ceiling fans in each bedroom, living area, and den. All the electrical wiring for the house was rewired, and all plumbing issues were repaired or replaced with new products. This was evident in the basement, where a new master bath was dug out by hand and installed with a beautiful bath to match the new bedroom that included a drop ceiling with can lights, new carpets and pad, a new walk-in closet and new paint to match.

Upstairs, the work continued, with the kitchen being gutted and new cabinets and counters and sink being installed. This was complemented by new furniture being provided, along with a wonderful gas fireplace installed by Dan Claxton of Claxton Fireplace in Omaha. Dan was able to provide extra heat to the basement, with venting downstairs from this new fireplace.

I then met a lady who asked to remain anonymous who worked at Westside Baptist Church in Omaha, and she was organizing something in our city called "Step Out." Step Out is an opportunity for churches all over the Omaha metro to work together one Sunday a year, often canceling local services to go work in the community. She was able to schedule a group of folks from her church to paint the whole exterior of the house and build a rather large deck in front. This was followed by a landscape company in Council Bluffs, Iowa, that donated plants for me and others to put in the ground strategically.

At the conclusion, we estimated that an $80,000 complete makeover had been shared and given to this family, without Sears or ABC, but simply using the talents, gifts, and abilities of so many within our community and local churches. It was an amazing blessing to behold and witness. It was not my networking skills that got this done, but rather the presence of God came and accomplished these tasks through many believers in our city and area.

I am sure I left out many wonderful details, but you get the gist of how this outreach and work of the ministry progressed. It was definitely a labor of love, with many donating time, money, and resources, yet never actually meeting the family or knowing them prior to helping, assisting, donating and installing. As with the story in chapter three about Peter being released from prison with the angel's help, we did our part and God did the rest.

Recently while driving to southwest Kansas with my son Jason, we stopped in a city park to rest and eat our lunch. After we ate, we noticed a lot of trash on the ground, so we just walked around and picked up as much as we could and placed it in the trash containers. No one saw us, and there was no reward or pat on the back. We just thought we would bless this small town with this random act of kindness and the opportunity to "do good" as Jesus modeled that for us.

Often, when staying with pastors or ministry leaders who are hosting me in their homes when I am ministering in their church, I look for ways to be helpful inside and out—especially outside. I have trimmed lots of trees and done some yard work for others as a gesture of kindness and gratitude for their hospitality. Sometimes this has entailed driving them to an appointment or perhaps doing some grocery shopping for them.

The point is that, even though I am a guest in a person's home, invited by the pastor to lead special services at that local church, this does not preclude me from serving, honoring, and blessing them when I indeed have the opportunity. I was taught years ago by a spirit-filled Lutheran pastor named Herb Mirly that to lead is to serve. This same ideal was instilled in me by my parents, who promoted that idea that any job worth doing was worth doing right and that excellence was a standard that was to be adhered to by our family. My personal friend Ed Silvoso teaches that labor with excellence is a form of worship.

Sometimes, the opportunity does not lend itself, due to a complicated schedule or some other conflict, but often I am able to share and encourage in a variety of ways. First Peter 3:9 says we have a calling to bless others. A calling is similar to an occupation, invitation, summons, or commandment to carry out a task or assignment. We literally have an assignment from God to serve and bless others, thus helping them to experience Jesus in the flesh, which in turn may open more doors for them to have a Kingdom Encounter. What an honor! What a privilege! Have you received your summons in this area yet?

Recently, our next door neighbors moved out, and whether intentionally or unintentionally, they failed to mow their grass. There was a one-day lag in time between when they moved out and the new neighbors moved in, so I decided to go over and mow the now rather tall blades of grass that had been growing unhindered for a couple of weeks, in hopes of just making the house welcoming for our new neighbors.

I had no idea when they might show up, so I was hurriedly mowing and had just about completed the lawn when they arrived. They immediately came over and thanked me, and we got acquainted. They were so happy to be in a friendly neighborhood. This early beginning of kindness and blessing has opened up other doors to share and be encouraging and has helped to maintain a good relationship with this young military couple. God knows where it is headed, but I am confident that taking the initiative in mowing has helped create an environment where the Holy Spirit has room to move and bring future godly impressions.

As I was writing this chapter, I started humming an old tune from when I was a teenager, which Burt Bacharach and Hal David wrote, composed, and titled "Alfie." This was later recorded by Cher and also Dionne Warwick. The lyrics really depict this godly theme I am writing about, and the words are here to challenge you.[7]

> What's it all about, Alfie?
> Is it just for the moment we live?
> What's it all about when you sort it out, Alfie?
> Are we meant to take more than we give,
> Or are we meant to be kind?
> And if only fools are kind, Alfie,
> Then I guess it's wise to be cruel.
> And if life belongs only to the strong, Alfie,
> What will you lend on an old golden rule?
> As sure as I believe there's a heaven above, Alfie,
> I know there's something much more,
> Something even non-believers can believe in.
> I believe in love, Alfie.
> Without true love we just exist, Alfie.
> Until you find the love you've missed you're nothing, Alfie.
> When you walk let your heart lead the way
> And you'll find love any day, Alfie, Alfie.

Notice that the lyrics say, "Without true love, we just exist." So many people just exist unto themselves, and until they discover the true love of the Father in the fullness of Jesus and completed by the comfort of the Holy Spirit, then all they do is just exist.

Existence is the state of having independent reality. But our reality as believers in Jesus is based on His true love that permeates our thinking, thus jump starting our actions and promoting Kingdom life to all we come into contact with. It no longer is about me, myself, and I. But rather, it is about Him. Jesus has become the agenda. And Jesus is our model. According to Acts 10:38, He went about "doing good," and so should we. By the way, as I write this, it is the Christmas season, and so often we hear that Jesus is the reason for the season, but let me hone that down a bit further and succinctly state that Jesus *is* the season. That really drives home the idea that it is indeed more blessed to give than to receive.

Because I currently travel in ministry, I see a lot of church life around the country and even the world, and to be honest, it is not all that pretty or exciting. There are indeed some amazing life-giving churches out there with incredible ministry that is radically changing the culture where they have and are establishing influence. Some of these churches are pretty small, and someday I may write about what I term "eight great little churches." Keep in mind that a megachurch should not be measured by numbers of people, but by influence.

But there are also some churches that are often uneventful and tied into boredom, with a lack of enthusiasm for anything spiritual. The Bible is clear when it declares that in the last days there will be a famine of the Word of God. In many of the places I travel, the people come up and share how hungry they are for what I just got finished teaching. And it is not the theme or subject that grabbed them, but just the infusion of the Word of God with an inclusion into their lives at that particular service. Infusion of the Word with inclusion of the people replaces the institution of the church with insightfulness and instrumentation of the Kingdom.

Instead of a solo pastor doing all the work of the ministry, we now have a symphony.

Infusion with inclusion brings impartation with immersion. In other words, as the Word of God is infused into us, it brings with it an impartation from the Holy Spirit that immerses us and saturates us into Kingdom thought, action, and lifestyle. We are changed from one form into another through this transformational process. There is indeed a great exchange that happens between God and us, and life as we previously knew it radically maneuvers into something brand new.

There is, in effect, a morphing that takes place. The transitive verb definition of the word *morph* deciphers this process with this definition: "To change the form or character of: transform; intransitive verb : to undergo transformation; *especially* : to undergo transformation from an image of one object into that of another." This is one of the main themes of the New Testament where transformation happens for anyone who encounters Jesus. Jesus is morphed into someone's life, and then that person indeed has a Kingdom encounter.

I've received a number of impartations in my life that literally changed how I did ministry and realigned me with what God was doing at that juncture and in that venture that created a new adventure in and with the Holy Spirit. When you add the anointing on top of that, you have a package that many people want, even though they don't yet know it. I am so honored to go to so many churches across the country and often experience what I will call "anointed afterglow." What I mean by that is that as the service concludes and the anointing was present, virtually no one wants to leave and go home or go out to eat. They tend to linger and visit, sometimes praying, while others just seemingly sit in amazement at what just transpired in their church. Many of the leaders notice it and can't quite get a handle on it, often commenting that they don't understand why no one is leaving. But I know why!

I remember ministering at a church in North Carolina, and the service began around 6 p.m. Everyone had been instructed to bring food to share for an extended snack time after the service. As the service was concluding around 8:00 p.m., the pastor announced to the congregation that it was time to move to the fellowship hall and enjoy the delicious snacks that everyone brought to share, but no one got up to leave. So he announced it a couple more times, but still no one wanted to leave, so he decided to ask the worship team to come back and lead some more worship, and this lasted another 90 minutes to 9:30 p.m., and then everyone just headed home.

What happened? There was an anointed afterglow that caused the people to want to linger, visit, and stay in God's presence, even if it meant giving up good physical food and fellowship. The fellowship with Jesus was so much sweeter, to the extent that no one wanted to leave. The imparting was more desired than the departing.

Without love, we just merely exist. Paul said in 1 Corinthians 13 that without love we really just make a lot of noise. But with the love of Jesus in our lives, we move from barely existing to expanding with expectancy to expedite and experience the Kingdom of God. This results in influence that motivates and saturates our spirit and our soul to the point that we simply don't care about anything else except serving the Lord. And this is often carried out by serving and blessing others.

Keep in mind that the word *influence* comes from the word *influenza*, which means to be in the flu. Most people reading this will understand that definition from a very practical point of view. But influence really means to be in the flow. We are to be in the flow of the river of God. As Ed Silvoso teaches, the difference between a river and a swamp is simply flow. And it is always good to be in a church that is flowing with the river of God.

Often, though, when serving and expanding the Kingdom, someone will come up and attack and blindside you to their thoughts that you are on the wrong track, or that perhaps you have overstepped your boundaries, and that you need to back off. They aren't afraid to let you know how wrong you are for whatever task you have been doing, and to then try to thwart your Kingdom activities and once again become self-centered to the point that you no longer are interested in expansion of God's Kingdom. If the enemy can get you to stop looking at Jesus long enough to look at your own problems, sins, and shortcomings, he has achieved his goal.

These attacks are similar to what happens in a swamp where all the animals devour one another. There is little life in a swamp, and what life is there is often thwarted and consumed by other animals. Some churches have this swamp mentality in which everyone is mad at each other. Whatever glimmer of life that sometimes appears is often sucked out by the un-anointed leeches that have risen up to ravage and pillage anything that may look godly, often in the name of tradition rather than with eyes that are seeking first the Kingdom of God.

The accuser of the brethren is the enemy of the cross and the enemy of the anointing of the Holy Spirit. Both of those power sources are so huge that the enemy uses intimidation, manipulation, and reminders of our past to get us to disconnect from those power sources, and then we are of no threat to him. He often uses people who don't have the same vision, tenacity of faith, and levels of spiritual influence to pull us down to their level—that somehow justifies their inadequacies and inabilities to move in the supernatural and in realms of faith. But I challenge you today: Don't listen to the critics. Don't respond to those who want to use the anointing for personal gain and who try to manipulate the Word of God to say something it was never intended to say.

I frequently use two verses when attacked, and they are Nehemiah 6:3 and Isaiah 54:17. Keep in mind that my overseers, accountability partners, and friends with a proven track record of hearing from God can speak into my life anytime they want, and I will certainly listen, thoughtfully reflect, pray, and usually make the necessary changes. But when people who know nothing about my life or my ministry come to me with the accusing finger of disrespect and dishonor me with attacking words, unsigned letters, obnoxious posts on blogs, and other media outlets, I simply respond with God's word in Nehemiah 6:3 and Isaiah 54:17. Read them below in context for a clearer understanding of what I am communicating here.

Nehemiah 6:1–9 states:

> Now it happened when Sanballat, Tobiah, Geshem the Arab, and the rest of our enemies heard that I had rebuilt the wall, and that there were no breaks left in it (though at that time I had not hung the doors in the gates), that Sanballat and Geshem sent to me, saying, "Come, let us meet together among the villages in the plain of Ono." But they thought to do me harm. So I sent messengers to them, saying, "I am doing a great work, so that I cannot come down. Why should the work cease while I leave it and go down to you?"
>
> But they sent me this message four times, and I answered them in the same manner.
>
> Then Sanballat sent his servant to me as before, the fifth time, with an open letter in his hand. In it was written:

Anointed Afterglow

It is reported among the nations, and Geshem says, that you and the Jews plan to rebel; therefore, according to these rumors, you are rebuilding the wall, that you may be their king. And you have also appointed prophets to proclaim concerning you at Jerusalem, saying, "There is a king in Judah!" Now these matters will be reported to the king. So come, therefore, and let us consult together.

Then I sent to him, saying, "No such things as you say are being done, but you invent them in your own heart."

For they all were trying to make us afraid, saying, "Their hands will be weakened in the work, and it will not be done."

"Now therefore, O God, strengthen my hands."

And Isaiah 54:11–17 reads as follows:

"O you afflicted one,
Tossed with tempest, and not comforted,
Behold, I will lay your stones with colorful gems,
And lay your foundations with sapphires.
I will make your pinnacles of rubies,
Your gates of crystal,
And all your walls of precious stones.
All your children shall be taught by the Lord,
And great shall be the peace of your children.
In righteousness you shall be established;

You shall be far from oppression, for you shall not fear;
And from terror, for it shall not come near you.
Indeed they shall surely assemble, but not because of Me.
Whoever assembles against you shall fall for your sake.

"Behold, I have created the blacksmith
Who blows the coals in the fire,
Who brings forth an instrument for his work;
And I have created the spoiler to destroy.
No weapon formed against you shall prosper,
And every tongue which rises against you in judgment
You shall condemn.
This is the heritage of the servants of the LORD,
And their righteousness is from Me,"
Says the LORD.

    I've experienced everything from recorded messages on phone calls, to being called the devil by a pastor, to having evil, unkind, and untruthful blogs written against me. I've been threatened with physical violence and called lots of names I can't print here. So I apply the principles of Nehemiah 6:3, which reveals that Nehemiah could not come down from building the wall and working the ministry of the Kingdom to contend with unfounded attacks. I also buckle the belt of truth with the words of Isaiah 54:17, declaring that any tongue that rises up in judgment against me I shall condemn, as this is not what my Father says about me or how He views me in righteousness.

    I once heard Jesse Duplantis share about how he was praying to God about some unjust actions and accusations coming his way, and how Jesus responded to him, stating that they spit on Him. Obviously, that is not the anointed afterglow that I am writing about here, but it is a good reminder that in our attempts to follow Jesus and step out to help and assist others, the religious crowd will probably get angry. The enemy will use those people to try to disengage us from our call to bless, encourage, love, and serve.

The Kingdom of God is kind of like franchising Heaven on earth. From McDonald's to Holiday Inn, from GNC to Hobby Lobby, and from Pet Smart to Great Clips, we see various types of franchises all based on and reflective of the parent company, including rules and regulations, uniforms, menus, health insurance plans, color schemes, signage, training, and marketing. All have to have the parent company's stamp of approval. Sometimes it's even the leaders of a church who let that religious spirit rise up and respond in an ungodly way. Some churches are deacon-possessed and truly need deliverance. I'm just saying.

The Kingdom of God functions in the same capacity with those of us engaged in the franchise receiving our marching orders and company policy from Heaven, but there will always be some who come attacking trying to get us to disenfranchise ourselves and thus lose our corporate identity that is so heavily tied to our CEO, Whose name is Jesus.

When the swamp monster emerges from the deep and tries to take you out, kill you off, or at the very least render you inactive, what will be your response?

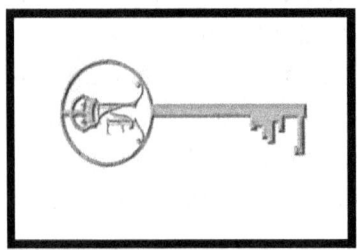

Kingdom Key #4: Look for ways to bless and serve!

As I was getting ready to conclude this chapter, I took a break from writing to go out and shovel some freshly fallen snow off my driveway, walkways, and deck. I noticed that my neighbor across the street, who is a widower and probably in his upper-70s, had only cleaned his driveway but not his walks. My initial thought was that since it is only 9 degrees and I had already worked a long time, I would just quit and go in for now since I know he has a snowblower. I do too, but mine is called a shovel, and it is manually powered. Even though my neighbor lives on an extended corner with sidewalks that I estimate to be three times as long as mine, I decided I would go over and extend this avenue of kindness.

I was going to write that this was a random act of kindness, but determined instead that it is rather intentional. Proverbs 12:2 declares, "A good man obtains favor from the Lord, but a man of wicked intentions He will condemn." I found that verse in Proverbs after I shoveled his walks.

Look for ways this week to have good intentions as it relates to serving and blessing others. Don't look for the easy way out, but instead anticipate that God wants to use you in incredible ways that will later give you opportunities to expand the Kingdom and advance the message of the gospel. The gospel is, after all, good news, is it not? Recently at a restaurant, the waiter failed to add to our bill a specialty iced tea, and I could easily have walked out without paying for it, but the obvious and truthful fact is that I could not have easily done this at all, so I let him know, and he corrected the bill to include the tea. Good intentions must be coupled with good integrity. Intentions with integrity influence increasing impartations from God.

Be a good and faithful steward of what it means to be a follower of Jesus! I am confident that both you and God will be glad you did. And don't let others convince you that you are on the wrong track, and especially don't let others try to take you down into the swamp.

Cherish these warnings and answers from Psalm 69, paraphrased in the Message Bible as follows:

> Quicksand under me, swamp water over me; I'm going down for the third time.

> Rescue me from the swamp. Don't let me go under for good, pull me out of the clutch of the enemy; this whirlpool is sucking me down. Don't let the swamp be my grave, or the Black Hole. Swallow me, its jaws clenched around me. Come close, God; get me out of here.

> Rescue me from this deathtrap. Let me shout God's name with a praising song. Let me tell his greatness in a prayer of thanks.

Chapter Five

Praying the Price in Public

I posted this on my Facebook page today because, as I write this, it is only two weeks until Christmas: "We receive Him by giving! Let every heart prepare Him room. Prepare to give, thus proving you have received Him!"

Romans 1:8–10 says, "First, I thank my God through Jesus Christ for you all, that your faith is spoken of throughout the whole world. For God is my witness, whom I serve with my spirit in the gospel of His Son, that without ceasing I make mention of you always in my prayers, making request if, by some means, now at last I may find a way in the will of God to come to you."

Ephesians 1:15–17 adds, "Therefore I also, after I heard of your faith in the Lord Jesus and your love for all the saints, do not cease to give thanks for you, making mention of you in my prayers: that the God of our Lord Jesus Christ, the Father of glory, may give to you the spirit of wisdom and revelation in the knowledge of Him."

First Timothy 2:1–3 multiplies it further: "Therefore I exhort first of all that supplications, prayers, intercessions, and giving of thanks be made for all men, for kings and all who are in authority, that we may lead a quiet and peaceable life in all godliness and reverence. For this is good and acceptable in the sight of God our Savior."

One of the easiest things to really give away is our time. And yet, that is also one of the easiest excuses to use when turning down an opportunity to help someone, simply by responding, "I don't have time."

Isaiah 44:8 shares this idea: "Do not fear, nor be afraid; have I not told you from that time, and declared it? You are My witnesses." Being a witness takes time. There just is no other way to describe the commitment that is involved. I'm sure you've heard it said that time is of the essence. I learned from Wikipedia that the phrase, *time is of the essence*, "is a term in British and United States contract law, which indicates that the parties to the agreement must perform by the time to which the parties have agreed if a delay will cause material harm."[8]

Being a witness in public, often including praying and ministering, does take time, yet I have frequently discovered that time was of the essence. It was not my time that might have been disturbed because of a delay, but rather the person with whom I was praying could have been greatly affected by certain delays. That is not always the case, but it has proven to be true. Let me illustrate.

This past summer, while checking in at the Delta counter in the Houston airport, getting ready to fly home after a great weekend of ministry in Texas, I struck up a conversation with the lady behind the counter. I was looking for a way to weave God into the conversation. At one point I was able to do that, which in turn opened a door for me to ask her if I could pray for her. She was delighted to receive my offer, and I asked her if there was something specific she wanted me to pray about. She simply asked that I pray that the passengers would not be so rude to her. She went on to explain that the majority of passengers that she waits on each day are either obnoxious or extremely rude and unkind to her, and that she would welcome some folks on the opposite end of the spectrum.

So I launched into my prayer for her, with her request as a primary focus, and then also included a few other things that came to my mind. When I was finished, she genuinely thanked me and said I was the nicest person to come up to her counter in weeks. She wanted to do something nice for me, so she offered to upgrade

Praying the Price in Public

me to first class for my flight. I then offered one more prayer that went something like this: "Thank you, Jesus!"

After I went through security, I headed to a newsstand to get some sugar-free gum. Once again, I struck up a conversation with the sales lady. During the conversation, she opened up about how her brother recently passed away and how sad she had been feeling. I brought some words of comfort and then offered to pray for her too, which she readily agreed to. After my prayer, she thanked me and said that God had told her that morning that He was going to bring her someone that day to comfort her, and she believed I was that person.

You may remember that back in chapter three I wrote about a set time, and for this lady at the newsstand, it was indeed a set time moment. To be honest, my courage level was way up after praying for the lady at the Delta baggage check in counter. What happened? I think I started being the lightning bug that I wrote about in chapter one. I remember texting my intercessory team in Omaha to let them know I was now having church in the Houston airport. God was working, and I was His coworker.

First Corinthians 3:9 says that we are called God's fellow workers. My pastor, Jim Hart, frequently reminds us that we are Jesus in the flesh. We have opportunities on a daily basis, and many of those opportunities only take time.

I really like the 1 Timothy passage earlier in this chapter, which lays it out quite plainly. You and I are to pray for people, both leaders and followers, whenever we can, wherever we are, and in whatever circumstances we find ourselves. Sometimes, those prayers are obviously quiet and sensitive to the moment, but more often than not, they provide an opportunity for others to experience God in ways that might never happen otherwise. We become God's conduit to release power on the earth that is readily available in Heaven right now. Theology and theophany blend together for an encounter.

To summarize, we have a job to do, and it includes prayer and intercession. I am definitely using the word *intercession* as another form of prayer here, but let me expound on it a bit further by breaking the word intercession into two forms.

"Inter" simply means to go into, and "cession" means to surrender. So with intercession, we are formulating and strategizing ways to help others go into and surrender to God's ways of doing things. There is a higher way with a higher power, and we have access to that power because we have previously surrendered to His Kingdom.

In Luke 17:20–21 we can learn from the words of Jesus that declare, "Now when He was asked by the Pharisees when the kingdom of God would come, He answered them and said, 'The kingdom of God does not come with observation; nor will they say, "See here!" or "See there!" For indeed, the kingdom of God is within you.'"

It certainly would be nice if we could just look at things, and God would suddenly and miraculously make things happen. But God makes it clear in these verses that the Kingdom of God does not come merely with observation. We don't get the option just to observe things and hope that someone else comes along to step in where we did not have enough courage or, God forbid, gave the excuse that we did not have enough time. We have a mandate to pray, bless, and encourage, and we have been given those marching orders, along with a vast and unlimited supply of Kingdom power, authority, love, joy, and a host of other godly attributes truly to make a difference in the lives of others.

From the December 2013 issue of the church newsletter from Beautiful Savior Lutheran Church in La Vista, Nebraska, where my good friend Keith Grimm is the Senior Pastor, comes these words from an article penned under the title of "How would you define the Gospel?":[9]

Praying the Price in Public

> Because we already possess everything we need in Christ, we can take great risks, push harder, go farther, and leave it all on the field without fear. We can invest with reckless abandon . . . The Gospel alone liberates us to live a life of scandalous generosity, unrestrained sacrifice, uncommon valor, and unbounded service.

You are liberated to pray with and minister to total strangers. You are free to encounter the Kingdom of God at home, while on the job, studying at school, swimming in a pool while on vacation, eating dinner at your favorite restaurant, and an endless variety of other places too. Luke 4:18 depicts part of the anointing that is upon us is for declaring liberty to those who are in captivity.

My friend, Pastor Duaine Johnson, who is the pastor of Purpose Church in St. Louis, has a wonderful teaching on the difference between bondage and captivity. Duaine has documented this in a great message, and he has sent me some notes to share with you here. Pastor Duaine searched and studied this topic biblically, and the Lord started showing him the two different yet closely related struggles of His people in the Old Testament. Of course, the understanding even translates to believers today. So here's what He started revealing in a broad stroke:

> Although Israel fought many battles, the two major enemies were Egyptians and Babylonians. These enemies were not like others who had victories here and there for certain numbers of years. These two managed to defeat the people of God well beyond physical beating. They not only outmuscled them, but they also broke their spirit and created strongholds in their minds. They affected the entire

lifestyle of the Lord's people, transforming their culture.

Egypt produced a victory resulting in 430 years of bondage (which in Hebrew means bitter work of any kind). Bondage was laborious, back-breaking, struggle-filled torment, in which Pharaoh determined their assignment. Their God-determined destiny was not being lived because they lived the world's bitter assignment. One thing it speaks to is the power of sin or a life outside the path of God. It's a life in which one is chained to something harsh or living an assignment that is bitter. It is blatant demonic attack. It is not subtle in the least. In fact, in bondage, the enemy thrives on fear. His success predicates upon public displays of force. People are being forced into roles that are nowhere close to their God-given DNA.

Yet this is the "early stage" of enemy attack. It's a very belligerent, juvenile system of the devil. The reason is those affected can tell it is bondage. This is a "good" thing, in a sense. The sheer fact they can feel the pressure and weight of the bondage brings them to a place where they cry out to be free. This is completely opposed to the struggle of Babylon. It is entirely different.

Babylon is not bondage; Babylon is captivity. In bondage you can feel the "whip" on your back, or in modern times, the bitterness in your soul from labor you are not designed to fulfill. However, in Babylon people are not bound to bondage they are "captive" in captivity.

Babylon thrives on the people of God being "captive." In other words, the influence of their captivity is in captivating the soul. This is not juvenile; this, in fact, is sophisticated. Now the enemies don't thrive on blatant acts but subtle deception *[remember my (Jay's) rattlesnake deception in chapter two]*. As a result, even though the things people do are still not according to the will of God, they are desensitized to it. The enemy works in deception and in desensitizing people. The scheme is to create a pseudo form of "freedom." The thought is, "Let's make people feel free, so they stay captive to the idea of intellectual life outside the confines of God's direction."

Its origins are traced to Nimrod. Nimrod hunted people. Nimrod thrived on the idea that to get "up," it was okay to put others down. This is still the core of Babylonian captivity. It's the "old" corporate ladder.

Think about this for a minute. Under the authority of Egypt, God's people were forced to stay and afraid to leave. *[My friend Jack Taylor, who wrote the foreword to this book, once stated that he remembered a man who swallowed an egg. He was afraid to move for fear it might break, and he was afraid to stay still thinking that it might hatch.]*

Under Babylon's rule, they are eventually allowed to leave, yet they are so comfortable that many stay. Even when they leave physically, Israel doesn't become what it was designed to be, partially because they left captivity but captivity didn't leave them (mentally). They were educated and taught to embrace the culture to the point they bought into this "freedom."

Even the hardest sinner will look to God with the whip of bondage on their back. But even the most spiritual have to be careful to not get lulled into being comfortable in captivity. It is a captivity of the mind built on the sophisticated pseudo-freedom of Babylon.

There are differences that go on for so long, yet I know this is a short description! In Egypt they all bake bricks and do not have distinct identity. In Babylon they like the diversity of people and thrive on making you another cog in the wheel, while making you feel important although still unfulfilled.

One of the Bible passages that deals expressly with captivity is 2 Corinthians 10:4–6:

> For the weapons of our warfare are not carnal but mighty in God for pulling down strongholds, casting down arguments and every high thing that exalts itself against the knowledge of God, bringing every thought into captivity to the obedience of

Christ, and being ready to punish all disobedience when your obedience is fulfilled.

Notice that God enables you to take control and bring negative arguments into captivity about why you can't pray for others or why you can't minister to others, and then all those negative thoughts are then brought into captivity, so that you are not captivated by the idea of the enemy that you can't do these things. The prominent idea here is that since you are reading this book, you desire to learn about and then walk in Kingdom encounters on a regular and consistent basis. To do that, you are stockpiling this "ammunition" in your arsenal of spiritual weapons, being ready with an answer in season and out.

Second Timothy 4:2 challenges us with these words: "Preach the word; be instant in season, out of season; reprove, rebuke, exhort with all long suffering and doctrine."

Couple that with 1 Peter 3:15 out of the KJV: "But sanctify the Lord God in your hearts: and be ready always to give an answer to every man that asketh you a reason of the hope that is in you with meekness and fear."

So, I will paraphrase. We are to take every negative non-Kingdom thought captive, predicated by preaching the Word, praying for others, in season and out, with a sanctified heart that is set apart to give an answer about the hope of Jesus in our lives and what He can do for others. This is our mandate from God.

And in the process, we actually make a difference in the lives of others as we contribute in a timely way, simply responding to what we see the Father doing, as is so aptly illustrated in John 5:19. Recently, I had a delivery for some lumber and deck materials, as we were expanding our backyard deck. I struck up a conversation with the driver of the truck, and to be honest, we weren't talking about anything spiritual or religious at all. But out of the blue, he just blurted out that the day before, when making a delivery, he had stepped in a hole and really wrenched his foot, and his foot and ankle were in a lot of pain.

I jumped on that one expeditiously, giving a couple of quick examples of how God had healed others. I then asked if I could pray for him. He quickly said, "Yes," and bowed his head for prayer. I literally prayed for twenty seconds or less, just inviting the presence of God at the curb and speaking healing. After saying, "Amen," I asked him if he could check it out. I told him that there is often a miracle when you check. So I encouraged him to walk to the back of his flatbed truck and then back to me. He had an obvious limp as he walked, but when he got to the rear of the truck, he turned around with a huge smile on his face, trotted back to me exclaiming that all of the pain had suddenly disappeared. He then thanked me repeatedly, got in his truck and waved as he drove away.

What happened? Remember, the Kingdom of God is within you and does not come by observation. I could have responded by saying I was sorry or that I hoped it would get better, but instead, I offered to pray, with the anointing that is upon me to set the captives free. He went away free from the pain and the limp. That's what God was doing, and I got to do it with Him as a fellow worker. Wow!

A couple of days later, I was working in the front yard when I started talking to a lawn guy who was working at my neighbor's house. I steered the conversation around to the Kingdom and asked him if he needed any prayer. He said he was concerned about the government shutdown at that time and how that might affect his social security check, so I prayed with him about that in my front yard and then went into a couple of financial testimonies. These prompted him to ask what I did for a living, and I shared some about my ministry. He then asked if I could share another story. This actually led to several more Kingdom stories, and he told me what local church he attends, but that he had not

Praying the Price in Public

heard these kinds of stories and was fascinated to learn that God works this way.

What happened? He went from having some religious experiences to having some Kingdom ones. Ecclesiastes 8:4 declares that where the Word of the King is, there is power. It's as if the lawn guy and the delivery truck driver both experienced a Kingdom power surge that strengthened and promoted something significant in their lives. The funny thing is that a few days prior to this, a man from the Omaha Public Power District came by to talk to me about reducing some electricity with my heat pump, and I ended up praying for him too. He was encouraged because of some personal issues that I touched on in my prayer, without knowing the circumstances. There was an obvious difference that day between God's power and manmade power sources.

Proverbs 15:33 in the Message Bible tells us that we get to experience the glory of God. Remember Isaiah 60:1 tells us that the glory of God rises on us, rather than descends to us. We carry the presence of God, and the Kingdom does not come by observation, but by responding to what we see the Father doing, and then leaping in with both feet to be a part of the action. In the book of Daniel, we learn that those who know their God are strong and take great action. If you know God, you are not some weak, anemic Christian. Your name is written in the Lamb's Book of Life, and you possess anointed power. You walk in glory and victory, and you are seated with Christ right now in heavenly places. Your position is one of authority with a winning attitude and motivation that says you can indeed do all things through Christ who strengthens you. You are victorious!

One of my teachings deals with being contagious with God. In the natural, touching and/or breathing on someone often takes what you may be contagious with and gives it to them. Poison ivy can be given to someone simply by touching that person with your infected hand. Maybe that is one principle that applies to Mark 16, where it says that sick people will become well when you lay hands on them and pray. Some diseases are received through airborne particles because of breathing. Perhaps there is a reason Jesus breathed on His disciples and said, "Receive the Holy Spirit."

Prayer is a great way to release what we have in a positive, contagious way. Being a contagious Christian is a topic that will be featured in my next book. We can literally influence the spiritual climate and atmosphere around someone else with spoken, faith-filled prayers. Recently, while on a trip to Michigan, I had two quick opportunities to pray with two different ladies. One had pain in her knees, and the other had what was the equivalent of a pinched nerve in her back. Both prayers did not last more than fifteen seconds. I distinctly invited the presence of God into the room and their situation, speaking healing, followed by asking them to check things out, leading to the discovery that both were healed completely from the constant pain they had been experiencing.

My God is good! He is a Healer and He is always in a good mood, because He is love, and He's got more than that loving feeling. His love is not based on a feeling, but on the reality of Jesus Christ and the finished work of the cross now manifested by and through the power of the Holy Spirit here on earth, as we agree with the Scriptures that say, "Thy Kingdom come. Thy will be done on earth—right now, where you are on earth—as it already is in heaven." Even if you are flying while you read this, you are under the authority of the law of gravity of this earth, which keeps you encased within the earth's atmosphere, so you qualify to receive Kingdom benefits right now.

One day, I was having lunch with a friend at Cheddar's restaurant, and during the meal, my friend shared that he was going to the doctor that afternoon, as he had a lot of pain on the bottom of one of his feet. I suggested to him that when we leave the restaurant, I could pray for him. He agreed. When we got outside, there was a bench by the curb, so I asked him to sit down and take off his shoe. I then prayed for his foot and asked him to walk across the crosswalk with his shoes off. He did and said that there was hardly any pain. So I prayed again, and he walked again, and the pain diminished even further. He called me that afternoon to tell me that he had canceled the doctor's appointment because the pain was totally gone. Isn't that remarkable?! God likes to heal people at restaurants too.

First John 1:2–4 gives us this incredible narrative from the Message Bible:

> From the very first day, we were there, taking it all in—we heard it with our own ears, saw it with our own eyes, verified it with our own hands. The Word of Life appeared right before our eyes; we saw it happen! And now we're telling you in most sober prose that what we witnessed was, incredibly, this: The infinite Life of God himself took shape before us.
>
> We saw it, we heard it, and now we're telling you so you can experience it along with us, this experience of communion with the Father and his Son, Jesus Christ. Our motive for writing is simply this: We want you to enjoy this, too. Your joy will double our joy!

And that is the truth, because, as I have shared in story after story, while ministering in other churches and in other states, I have received so many emails and letters sharing with me how my stories of Kingdom life and adventure have sparked new and renewed interest in presenting the gospel in public. These testimonies and stories really do double my joy.

Discipleship is one of my favorite ministry goals, and to see and hear about others who are doing great exploits for God is an amazing blessing. I've had children, youth, and adults share personal stories, stating how amazed they were when God showed up, and what an honor it was to pray for someone, download a personal word of knowledge or wisdom, or pray a prayer for healing and actually see the individual who was being prayed for get well. They loved it! And I was so happy! These simple tasks often help move people out of bondage and captive situations into true, eventful encounters with the Lord.

For me, I am hooked on Jesus and hacked off at the devil. The devil has won far too many battles simply because Christians did not show up. I learned long ago that emotion will get you to sign up but commitment gets you to show up. I think it is time for all of us to begin to show up on a consistent basis. Bondages are broken and captivity is taken captive through the cross of Jesus. The Kingdom of God does not come through observation.

Remember, as we run the race, it is not a sprint but a marathon. God will use us to expand and promote His Kingdom, thus demonstrating His power through us to others, who in turn can show His power to more and more people, until everyone has heard, and many are flowing in personal and corporate revival. But we must be willing to step out in faith and take the chance. God has never failed to come through for me when I took that initial step. Faith can be spelled RISK, but I will deal more on that subject in chapter seven.

Praying the Price in Public

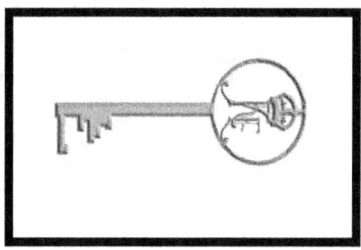

Kingdom Key #5: Now is the time.

My son Jason has released a worship album called *Running Free* and in it are a number of original songs, including this one called "Now is the Time." Read the words below for yourself, and then read them again, thinking about someone you know who needs prayer. Then take time to pray for them before going on to the next chapter. Listen closely to what the Lord may tell you to do while you are praying too. He may surprise you!

Now Is the Time[10]

Now is the time of the favor of the Lord
Now is the time when all hope will be restored
And though the road is rough and the journey's hard
This is the time

Now is the time when your dreams will be fulfilled
Now is the time when God's enemies are stilled
And what you're longing for—
what you're praying for
This is the time

This is the time when the longing hearts
Will find peace in love, will find hope in God
This is the time when the thirsty soul
Will be filled again—let revival fall

On this dry and thirsty land
Lord, we need Your touch again
Restore us, renew us, revival fall
Lord, our only hope is You
Let us never thirst again, Oh, Lord.

Chapter Six

The Un-Young Renewed Youth Minister

A good friend of mine that I met on the New Wine email list invited me to Los Angeles to minister to some students at her high school. My friend's name is Pia, and she is a high school teacher who was able to pull a lot of strings to get me to come and speak to high school students from several public high schools in the Glendale and Los Angeles area. When I arrived, I discovered that most of the students were Korean, with some who were Black, White, and Hispanic. Fortunately, I love cultures, so I blended in nicely. Well, okay, I am exaggerating a bit on the blending in part, because I was substantially taller than most of the students at this event. But still, after being with them for three days, they begged me to stay and launch a youth church in that area. Can you imagine a guy in his mid-fifties launching a youth church?

I am always amazed that God will use me to speak to young people and that they will actually listen to me, because as I stated, I am in my mid-fifties. Yet, I usually lead between twenty and thirty youth and student events every year. How is that possible? I will share that in a moment, but first let's go back to the L.A. story.

The weekend was amazing, and I personally saw nearly 100 students get right with God. One afternoon, with just the youth leaders in attendance, the Holy Spirit came in a powerful way, with manifestations and healings happening all over the room. God showed up BIG TIME, and it truly was an incredible move of the Holy Spirit, with joy, hunger for more of God, carpet time, healings, and other manifestations of God being enjoyed by those in the room who entered into and lingered with the presence of the Lord. (For those of you who don't know what "carpet time" is, please read chapter thirteen called "There Goes One," in my book *Willing to Yield*.)

Near the end of the weekend, during some anointed prayer ministry that was happening, a group of cheerleaders approached me for prayer, stating that they were in the state championship coming up and that they wanted prayer for that event. I noticed that one of the girls seemed to be limping, and I was informed that she had fallen and twisted her ankle. It was causing her considerable pain. I asked her if I could pray for her, and she sighed rather loudly, responding, "I guess so." I then asked her again to be sure it was okay, and she sighed again, rolled her eyes a bit and simply nodded her head.

So I began my prayer for the group and then turned the prayer emphasis toward this girl and her twisted ankle, speaking healing and sharing words of faith. I then suggested that she walk toward the other end of the room where there was a table, and I urged her to walk around the table and come back to me. She sighed again and asked, "Do I have to?" I said no, she did not have to, but I felt like God would do something special for her if she did. She sighed again and rolled her eyes again, shrugging, but she agreed to do it.

I am sure there were at least two significant things happening simultaneously. First, she was in obvious pain, and walking sounded like a huge chore; but second, I was pretty confident she did not have a relationship with Jesus, thus the sighing aspects continued.

Anyway, off she went, limping across this rather larger room. When she got to the table and rounded it, she had a huge grin on her face, and she literally trotted back, practically shouting at us in a gleeful voice that all of her pain had totally disappeared.

The Un-Young Renewed Youth Minister

At this point, it was pretty easy to introduce her to Jesus as her Savior, Lord, and very best friend.

Some of the coolest testimonies come when children, students, and young adults are engaged in Kingdom ministry and Kingdom life. I frequently remind myself of the great responsibility I have when ministering to youth and students. I have been so honored to minister to children in grades K–5, middle school children in grades 6–8, high school students in grades 9–12, and yes, even university students too. I am so happy to teach, share, pray with, and release the power of God over and into students of all ages, many of whom have only experienced a religious Jesus, but not the One Who truly is real and alive today.

Listed directly below is a testimony written by Jeni Langfeldt, as she observed some unique things happen with and to the students she was responsible for.

> I have witnessed Pastor Jay West receive multiple downloads from Heaven. While a teacher at a Christian school, every year I carried on the tradition of organizing and taking my students on a three-day, two-night outdoor education experience. We ventured to a camp within our state and did various activities like: archery, navigating with compasses, fishing, horseback riding, dissecting owl pellets, cooking in Dutch ovens, riding on zip lines, and other exciting things! This annual experience was always a major highlight for the sixth, seventh, and eighth grade students at my school.
>
> One year, I invited Pastor Jay and his son Jason to come minister to my students while at camp. I kept it a secret from them until the event was to take place. It was a powerful experience and one that I

am sure none of my students will forget for the rest of their lives!! After an awesome time of teaching, Jay began to pray for each of my students. They were lined up in front of the outdoor altar in a single horizontal line. He began at one end and spent time with each student until everyone had been prayed for. Jay had met my students before, but he didn't know any of them on a personal level. As he prayed for each student, I watched as the Holy Spirit spoke specifically to each one. Silent tears began to roll down their cheeks. Jay had no knowledge of the details of any of my students there that evening, but I did (as I had been their teacher for 1–3 years each). As he prayed, I listened to each one, and the "downloads" he received "hit the nail on the head" for each one! It was amazing!!

I can't remember everything he said that night, but one stands out in my mind: Jay prayed for a sixth grade boy who was being raised by a single mom. The father was in and out of jail, barely around for his son and physically abusive to his mother. This student struggled with lying, cheating and stealing. (I had caught him doing all three of these things.) He was small in stature and took medication for ADHD. In the classroom, he loved attention. This usually resulted in him trying to be funny at inappropriate times. Pastor Jay began by praying for this student, and he then received a download that went something like this: "You wear a smile on your face, and you like to make others laugh. You might even be called the 'class clown,' but that is really a mask to hide your pain, isn't it?" At this point, tears rolled down his cheeks and he nodded his head. Jay then hugged him and prayed for him.

I was in awe! Jay didn't know one thing about this child's history or current situation. I was thanking and praising God that he loved each of my students so much that He would use Pastor Jay to speak something so specific to each one! When Pastor Jay was done praying, all my students stayed in the outdoor chapel and began praying for each other!! That too was a miracle! Had I not seen it for myself, I wouldn't have believed it. They were huddled together crying, praising God, and fervently praying for one another!! It was all GOD! I overheard some of my students saying, "This was the best surprise! This was the best part of outdoor education!" Remember, this is what they said in comparison to horseback riding and zip lining through the trees! Nothing can compare to being in the presence of our God! *[This is called anointed afterglow!]*

There have actually been occasions when I was influential with youth who had never previously been in church before. In America, that seems hard to fathom, yet it is true. Yet God still loves these kids just as much as anyone else, and His love flows towards them in amazing, unending, significant ways that draw them toward a new life in and with Jesus.

Let's read some of Psalm 103. Here are verses 1–5 and then 19:

> Bless the LORD, O my soul;
> And all that is within me, bless His holy name!
> Bless the LORD, O my soul,
> And forget not all His benefits:
> Who forgives all your iniquities,
> Who heals all your diseases,
> Who redeems your life from destruction,
> Who crowns you with loving kindness and tender mercies,
> Who satisfies your mouth with good things,
> So that your youth is renewed like the eagle's.
>
> The LORD has established His throne in heaven,
> And His kingdom rules over all.

I love it that God's Kingdom rules over all. His position is supreme, and His power is supernatural. And I like the idea that my personal youth is being renewed. Isn't that a wonderful benefit of knowing God? I can't prove that is happening, as I accept it by faith; but it sure explains why a guy with graying hair continues to get invitations to speak to students and youth of all different ages. It also seems to figure into the equation of why these students would listen to me and then respond like they do. Let me share an example.

I was invited to speak at a chapel service at a local Christian school for middle school students. When I walked in, there were about 125 middle school students bouncing off the wall. Most of them were talking excitedly and loudly, and even the acoustic guitar-playing worship leader had problems getting them

The Un-Young Renewed Youth Minister

to sing. In my estimation, about twenty-five percent were involved in those initial songs, and the rest either just watched or continued to talk.

Later, the administrator of the school shared with me and his faculty that, after my introduction, I had them from the first words out of my mouth. I honestly don't remember what I talked about that day, but I can tell you this: That thirty-minute chapel lasted nearly three hours. There was a lot of personal prayer ministry, crying, and repenting. At the conclusion, those 125 junior high students were fully engaged in forty-five minutes of non-stop worship, many of them dancing, twirling, and kneeling, some with hands raised, but all fully participating and enjoying God's presence.

The next week I went back, and more of the same happened, but my theme was different, and some of the teachers were invited to come forward. There were periods of forgiveness being shared between staff and students as well as students and staff. It was a very touching and special moment. I remember one time I walked into a school chapel setting and taught and gave an invitation for those students to get right with God, and 72 students responded. The next week, I went back again, and without teaching or sharing, I simply launched with an invitation for more to get right with God who wanted to the week before but did not step forward. God told me there would be eleven who would respond, and you guessed it, eleven more young people accepted Jesus right there without any teaching, stories, or testimonies—just an immediate opportunity from the beginning. You know God is in the house when these things happen.

Most of the school administrators now honor my request to have two chapels in back-to-back weeks, and most will give me an hour to minister, rather than the normal twenty to thirty minutes that they usually have. For some reason, the Holy Spirit just comes, and the presence of God is so real, so tangible, and so amazing that these young people do not want to leave. They often linger, praying or asking questions. I get letters from parents and administrators telling me how amazed they are at the responses that happen. I am amazed too, but mostly amazed that Jesus allows me to do these things, and I get to see some pretty incredible moves of God.

You might be asking, what is my secret? I can tell you pretty easily. I don't have them read the Bible with me on my first visit. I do quote Bible passages and share interesting true stories, usually ones that include people who are in their mid-twenties and younger. I really only share personally experienced stories, and I normally keep my talks to about fifteen minutes or less. Then I invite the presence of the Holy Spirit in prayer, and He comes very quickly. The young people immediately start responding. I never have to wait, beg, or plead with them to get a response. God just moves on the right ones and the rest follow. I really don't care why they come forward for prayer, or what motivated them to respond, because I know God will meet them up front in supernatural ways. It is His supernatural combined with my testimonies and quoting of His Scriptures that gets them to want more of God. I just sandwich myself between God, and I can't lose. When praying, I often receive personal words of knowledge, which grab their attention all the more. I could probably write a whole book about these student and youth experiences. Remember, that God's natural is supernatural.

As I walked up to speak at one middle school chapel, I suddenly felt impressed by the Holy Spirit to pray for kids who had pain in their body. About thirty or forty students stood up, and as I prayed, I had them raise their hands if they felt the pain leaving. Literally in seconds, more than half of those standing were healed instantaneously. I would stop and let them share where they previously hurt, how that pain had come to them, and then what they were feeling. These middle school students would spontaneously applaud and bless God as His miraculous power was transforming the room and their viewpoint of what were often boring chapels. Nothing is boring when God shows up.

Some prayer ministry is more sensitive than others, so when it is a sensitive subject, I will just have these kids look at me with their eyes. No hand raising, no standing up—just an honest appraisal with a look that shows me that they have an immediate need. No one besides Jesus and me needs to know.

The following example has been used with youth and churches, but always with the leader's permission in advance. Whatever the talk is, I can use this example at the conclusion, but I only do it when I have God's backing. Otherwise, I stay away from it. I do not want to appear to be using a prop that is not authorized by the Lord, and I want those who experience this to gain the maximum benefit from the experience with God. I am opposed to methods but very open to the fresh leading of the Holy Spirit.

In 1 Corinthians 15, the Bible says that first comes the natural, and then the spiritual. So when that biblical principle is applied to these actions, incredible things often happen. What I do is, as I am concluding my talk, I walk around the room with a water bottle in my hand gently pouring some water into the palm of my hand and flinging that water into the air, which falls as mist on the heads of those in the audience. I normally speak for a while about how we come to church maybe to get a little sprinkle from God's river or a little touch, but not really being immersed. By this time, I am generally back to the front of the room, and I share that God really wants to douse us with his presence and saturate us with Himself. After I have securely taken off any cordless microphones, I then pour the remaining part of the water bottle over my head, and it drenches me. All the while, those who are watching begin to gasp or laugh or point, but they are definitely all engaged.

Like I said, I have done this with students and with adults, and for some reason the people quickly run to the front and they want me to dump water on them too. The room is always ecstatic with the Lord's presence, as this one simple, natural act is carried out. The spiritual applications of being in the river are also then released, and powerful ministry happens.

Healings, freedom of worship, people gathering for prayer, some repenting to each other, and a variety of other ministry aspects are released as the water is poured. Anointed prayers are included, and the power of God hits the room like a thunderstorm that unleashes its power in a torrential downpour. Many are physically healed as the water is poured over their heads. One chapel service in Iowa ended up lasting four hours. Another church in Minnesota received a new release of worship. I later got a letter from the pastor, stating he had never seen his people worship like they did after that natural and supernatural soaking time.

By the way, I need to thank my friend Shane Rootes for sharing this particular water bottle ministry example with me. Shane is a worship musician who used to travel with the group *Delirious?*, or the "D Boys," as he calls them. You can find Shane on my Facebook page if you want to connect with him, as he is a very anointed worship leader with a lot of risk-taking attitudes. One time I saw Shane lead a communion service, playing fast-paced songs on his cordless electric guitar while walking around the worship center. It was passionate, positive, and productive.

You may recall that Revelation 19:10 says that the testimony of Jesus is the spirit of prophecy, so when you and I hear a testimony, we need to reinforce this information and transformational thought from Revelation 19. Otherwise, we will simply hear the testimony and good report of what God has done, nodding our heads and maybe saying Amen, but not applying it to our lives for the moment. As James clearly articulates in chapter two of his epistle, hearing without doing anything has this pronouncement, which is setting yourself up to be deceived. Some of that advice was already discussed in chapter two.

The Un-Young Renewed Youth Minister

The password or connection here is to realize that a testimony becomes a prophetic word that has power attached to it that can then release something in our lives that we are believing for, even if not directly related to the testimony you just heard or read. All of my books, teachings, and presentations are packed full of testimonies, and these testimonies then become words of knowledge, words of wisdom, discernment, and prophecy for the present and the future so that the hearers can claim similar victories, similar steps to overcoming, similar miracles, and definitely similar signs and wonders for themselves based on what God did for another.

This literally is a magnificent sign and wonder available to everyone today. You don't have to believe in the supernatural for today. All you have to do is believe the testimony that you just heard is true, and God can take care of the rest. But it is obviously even more effective if you reach out, grab hold of that testimony in faith, pull it close to your heart, and whisper to God, "I want some of that." Luke 11:9–12 truthfully elaborates this to us with these words:

> So I say to you, ask, and it will be given to you; seek, and you will find; knock, and it will be opened to you. For everyone who asks receives, and he who seeks finds, and to him who knocks it will be opened. If a son asks for bread from any father among you, will he give him a stone? Or if he asks for a fish, will he give him a serpent instead of a fish? Or if he asks for an egg, will he offer him a scorpion? If you then, being evil, know how to give good gifts to your children, how much more will your heavenly Father give the Holy Spirit to those who ask Him!

God wants to give you more than you normally ask for, and He wants to come through for you just like He did for the person who is sharing the testimony. God really is a good Father.

Case in point, as I was sharing about some youth and student testimonies at a school one day, a young man who was in seventh grade came up to me afterwards and told me that all his youth group ever did was play volleyball, board games, and computer games. He stated that there was nothing spiritual happening at all, but he wanted to make a difference. I prayed with him for his request.

I met him a year or two later, and he began to tell me that he took my message of courage back to his youth group. Keep in mind that almost everyone attending that youth group was older than him, but he persisted, and now he was so excited to share with me that his youth group was involved in Bible study, outreaches, and prayer for others. Without an official youth leader or youth pastor, this seventh grade student took courage and stood up for the Kingdom. Incredibly, the youth group had also tripled in size and was doing amazing Kingdom things for the Lord. Yes, they still occasionally played various games, but now the focus was on Jesus. Now, that is more than wonderful, more than amazing, and more than fantastic. That is GOD! That is an encounter!

I was at a local Starbucks one day, and the young lady barista behind the counter recognized me and asked me if my name was Jay West. She went on to say that she remembered a time when I came to her school and shared at chapel. She could remember the story almost perfectly, and get this, it had been eight years since she had heard me. Yet she remembered the story and then she shared the impact it had on her life. This happened again at a local Wal-Mart, where a young man approached me and said he remembered when I had come to his school seven years prior and how much that particular chapel meant to him at the time. It even happened recently when I was at a local Christian bookstore, and a young lady approached me, telling me how much she had previously enjoyed my teaching and was hoping I would return to her church soon.

Hebrews 6:10 puts it this way: "For God is not unjust to forget your work and labor of love which you have shown toward His name, in that you have ministered to the saints, and do minister." Having people come up to me in public places, thanking me for ministry that happened several years prior, is such a tremendous encouragement. This usually happens on days when I really need that encouragement. As John Wimber used to say, "God gets the glory and we get the hugs." I like these kinds of hugs, don't you?

You need to understand that I personally really love discipleship. Seeing people grow in their faith and mature into on-fire-for-Jesus believers is a powerful exhibition of the Kingdom of God, and I love to experience and see those exhibitions first hand. But because I am currently in a traveling ministry position and have been for over twelve years now, I often feel more like a cheerleader than a coach. So when these young disciples come up to me and share how a message or perhaps a prayer helped change their life, it is a huge booster shot of faith pumping directly into my heart to stir me on for more of what God wants me to do. I have a message called "Do You Need a Faith Lift?" This is one such way that a faith lift comes—through the testimony of others.

Sometimes people come up and share with me about a healing that they experienced when I previously prayed for them, but I never heard the result. One such event happened just recently when I was inside a Big Lots store. An older lady approached me and asked my name, and then she recognized me and told me about something that had happened ten years prior. I remembered the story, but did not know the outcome. She had come to the service with a walker, and I prayed for pain issues to lessen, and then challenged people to do something that they could not do prior to the prayer. She laid her walker under the pew and walked forward without the aid of her walker. Her pain had left that morning.

What I did not know, but learned that day in Big Lots, was that she was a candidate for knee replacement surgery and was supposed to have had it within a month or so after that service. But because of the prayer and her stepping out in faith without the walker, she never had to have the knee surgery. Praise God! This was about ten years later that she was telling me this story, as it was the first time she had seen me since I had been at her church.

I would like to conclude this chapter with the verses in Hebrews 6:9–12. Let's read these out loud:

> But, beloved, we are confident of better things concerning you, yes, things that accompany salvation, though we speak in this manner. For God is not unjust to forget your work and labor of love which you have shown toward His name, in that you have ministered to the saints, and do minister. And we desire that each one of you show the same diligence to the full assurance of hope until the end, that you do not become sluggish, but imitate those who through faith and patience inherit the promises.

Don't you just love the Word of God? This passage alone is so rich and full of life and sustaining power. God wants us to be confident. Don't let someone's age, degree, or financial status impede your Kingdom adventure in presenting truth to that person. Don't be afraid, and don't back down from any assignment that God may want to give to you. God has plans that are so spectacular and often come to fruition years later at the precise moment that demonstrates His sovereignty and His care for us. God cares deeply for you and for those He has called you to minister to and care for. God wants to use you and me to reach the unreachable, touch the untouchable, and take the anointed gospel message and impartations to the sighing, crying, and dying humanity who are all

The Un-Young Renewed Youth Minister

around us. So many people desperately need a special touch from God.

In chapter one of *Dreaming with God* by Bill Johnson, his thoughts are shared:[11]

> There is no question that spending time with God changes our desires. We always become like the one we worship. But it's not because we've been programmed to wish for the things He wants us to wish for; it's because in friendship we discover the things that please Him—the secret things of His heart. It is the instinct of the true believer to search for and find, that which brings pleasure to the Father. Our nature actually changes at conversion. It is our new nature to seek to know God and to please Him with our thoughts, ambitions, and desires.
>
> Those who have the greatest difficulty with this line of thinking are those who consider this to be an assault on the doctrine of the sovereignty of God. There is no question; God is sovereign. But His position of ruler-ship is not denied by our assignment to co-labor with Christ. One of my favorite quotes on this subject comes from my dear friend Jack Taylor. He says, "God is so secure in His sovereignty that He is not afraid to appear un-sovereign."

I wanted to use this particular quote for two reasons. One, to add depth to my previous discussion and writing about being a coworker, or fellow worker, with Jesus. But also to share the quote in Bill Johnson's book by Jack Taylor, who has written the foreword to this book as well. Both Bill and Jack have a huge reservoir of faith, experience, and Godly anointed power that is filled to the brim with all the fullness of the Godhead bodily, as declared in Colossians 2:8–10 which announces:

> Beware lest anyone cheat you through philosophy and empty deceit, according to the tradition of men, according to the basic principles of the world, and not according to Christ. For in Him dwells all the fullness of the Godhead bodily; and you are complete in Him, who is the head of all principality and power.

There will be some who will try to tell you these powerful things don't happen anymore, or that their traditions don't allow for such a move of God. I am encouraging you to ask God about this, as He is truth, and He will present the truth to you in ways that only you will understand and appreciate.

Since the above quote was a longer quote, I wrote to Bill Johnson and received his permission to share it with you. I believe it is excellent and hope you will trust the significance of its meaning and apply the truth of the subject directly to your life today.

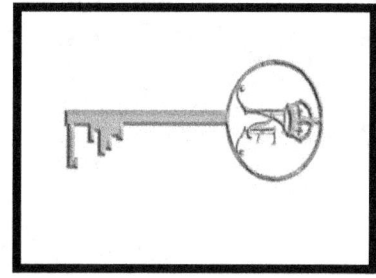

Kingdom Key #6: Time to trust.

Psalm 71:5 gives many of us an historical Kingdom viewpoint.

> For You are my hope, O Lord GOD;
> You are my trust from my youth.

In other words, you may be one who has heard years and years of sermons and messages, attended many Bible studies and seminars, yet you haven't really stepped out in faith to share about Jesus with anyone. It's kind of like the old joke about those who rarely go to the gym—that they only know it as James. If you have heard five good sermons and read some of your Bible, then you are ready to trust God and see how He may want to use you, especially with those outside of your comfort zones. And if you have known God most of or all of your life, then it is way past time to ask Him to use you immediately. You've been trusting Him a long time in other venues, so why not now?

The questions then become, if not now, then when; and if not you, then who? Spend a few moments right now and ask God to show you someone specific to begin to talk to about Jesus. He will show you the way and offer sound advice along the way. You can rely on the Holy Spirit because of the words of Luke 12:12,

"For the Holy Spirit will teach you in that very hour what you ought to say." As I have said before, trust is a must!

Take time to meditate on these two verses from Psalms 37:3 and 5.

> Trust in the LORD, and do good; Dwell in the land, and feed on His faithfulness.
>
> Commit your way to the LORD, Trust also in Him, And He shall bring it to pass.

Dwell and live there. I often encourage people who are going through hell not to get a motel there, and not to get a condo, but to keep moving. God will take you to His land where you can dwell and feed on his faithfulness, and what you are believing for, you will see come to pass.

Isaiah 26:3 proclaims this great blessing! "You will keep him in perfect peace, whose mind is stayed on You, Because he trusts in You." Now read this verse out loud several times until it is deep down in your spirit. I believe you will soon see and experience a difference that includes even peace. It is time to trust because trust is a must.

Chapter Seven

WOW! WOW! WOW!

My friend Dr. Ed Silvoso has a habit of proclaiming, "Wow, Wow, Wow," when something genuinely excites him, so I have titled this chapter with those same expressive words. My goal in this chapter is to wow you with the wows of God: manifestations, answers to prayer, and various activities of the Spirit that only God could have put together and arranged.

The ministry that I have been involved in for the past fourteen years is included in this wow encounter, as I am just not smart enough to have ministered in over sixty-two different denominations. I am not bright enough to have arranged to minister in over one hundred local churches in the greater Omaha area. It is amazing to me that so many astounding doors of opportunity have opened to me in the years we have lived here. To realize that I get to hang out with great pastors, authors, musicians, doctors, politicians, plumbers, roofers, landscapers, teachers, governors, senators, mayors, and Kingdom-minded folks on a regular and consistent basis is so wonderful to think about. I am so honored to get to speak to children, middle school students, and high school students, along with college-aged young adults.

Plus, I get to go to churches of so many different cultures and ethnicities. I just love being with people and learning from them as I get to teach and minister about the Kingdom of God. And then to write books that have been read in several countries, prisons, and in the homes of some very famous people, not to mention being read by you right now—I am so honored. This is just one of many wow situations in my life.

So here are a few wow moments that became wows of momentum through many years of ministry. Some of these appear in previous books but are so cool and worth repeating that they are included here for you to read and enjoy. Before you begin, though, let me remind you, as I mentioned in the previous chapter, that you should take the posture of Revelation 19:10, which declares that the testimonies of Jesus are the Spirit of prophecy. What this means is that the testimonies you are about to read are not really mine, but those of Jesus working in and through me. Beyond that, these testimonies are not meant to be read simply with a sense of joy and gladness for what God did through or for me, but rather with an expectancy and urgency, coupled with anticipation, knowing that what God has done with me, He can and also wants to do with you.

God's love is so inclusive and so expressive that He sincerely desires to share Himself with as many as possible and to assist you with whatever need, trial, hurt, difficulty, sickness, pain, suffering, financial obligation, or relational problem you are facing. His power is ready to be shared and released in your life easier than it is to plug an electrical cord into a wall socket and get common electricity for your appliance, tool, or entertainment source. Jesus has unending power and supply for whatever you presently need. I made this statement up many years ago, and it goes like this. Whatever God has, I need; and whatever I need, God has. So with that thought in mind, let's begin.

I have lots of healing testimonies that I love to share, and will write about a few here just to launch this section. I am very enthusiastic and spiritually charged when people get well right in front of me. Just this week, I had the opportunity to pray for a lady whose shoulder and arm were in desperate need of healing with all of the pain she was suffering. Where her arm connects to her shoulder, there was no ball joint or socket to hold the arm intact, and only some muscles and cartilage were actually holding the arm in place. She was scheduled to have some sort of replacement surgery in the near future, and she was in obvious pain as she came forward for prayer. I simply prayed that God would heal her and that the pain would disappear. She was not able to lift her arm more than three inches from her side, but after about thirty seconds of prayer, she could slowly, through tears of joy, lift her arm up to the top of her head. She later sent me a note on Facebook, sharing that she had no pain in her arm at all.

I have prayed for hundreds of people with various pains in their knees, legs, feet, and hands due often to arthritis, neuropathy, bursitis, and even cancer, who, after a short amount of prayer, were completely healed. Yes I have seen a few—not a lot—but a few lay down their walkers and canes and walk. I have seen a couple of people get out of wheel chairs and walk, sometimes running freely without those apparatuses being used. I have seen the effects of pain leave from young children and older adults.

One time at a local Lutheran church, the Lord instructed me to pray for those in the congregation who had pain in their feet, ankles, and knees. I asked those who were in those categories to stand up, and eight people stood to their feet. God told me to have them jump. I looked around and noticed that all of them seemed old, so I questioned God, asking, "Have you seen how old they are? Jumping on a good day would be a treat."

He simply responded back, "Have them jump." So I shared with the folks what the Lord had told me and that if they felt they had faith to jump, then they should go ahead, but if not no one would question their response. Before I could finish talking about this, some began to jump, and soon all eight were jumping up and down. Suddenly, several of them began to let out some shouts—joyful shouts—and I could tell that something was happening. Believe it or not, all eight were totally healed. Seven of them got immediate relief, while the last one woke up well the next morning. One lady was in her eighties and was the pastor's mother. She was scheduled for knee replacement surgery, yet seven years later when I met her again, she told me she never had to have the surgery. These are wow factors, for sure!

I was preaching at a conference once, and God stopped me in the middle of my message and told me to pray for people with eye problems. I do not remember how many stood up, but fifty-three people were healed of all sorts of eye disorders in less than three minutes. Several people came up to me repeatedly during the remainder of the conference to tell me that they had been healed. I find it amazing that we can pray for groups of people with similar problems and they get well without anyone laying hands on them or specifically praying just for them individually. God is so gracious and kind and loves for us to pray for groups of people and for those in multitudes. Some of the eye problems that I have personally seen healed are floaters and shooting stars, blurred vision, double vision, cataracts, glaucoma, macular degeneration, dry eyes, lazy eyes, and partial blindness. One time, when I was at a local Hispanic church, I prayed for a lady who could only read the big "E" on the eye chart, but after a short prayer, she stood in front of the congregation and read from her Bible, which was font size fourteen. At that same service, another lady had crippling arthritis in her hands, and we all watched in amazement as her fingers uncurled and she had no pain or discomfort in those fingers. Come on, Jesus!

I was honored to pray for a guy at a local restaurant who battled fibromyalgia, and God healed him by about fifty percent when I was with him. Then one week later, he was totally well. Still others have been healed with metal in their bodies. Metal is often surgically placed in bodies to provide support and relief from a serious injury or ailment, but then it manifests negatively with cold, numbness, and pain. I can't remember how many people have been healed of these negative manifestations because, again, I often pray for these folks in groups, and there are often so many people in a congregation who will have metal in their bodies either in joints, as pacemakers, or as screws, pins, and plates to hold

WOW! WOW! WOW!

things together. Many, many people have stood up to testify how the pain disappeared while I was praying. Still others give glory to God with emails and text messages of such healings, while others wait until I return to that congregation, sometimes years later, to tell me how they have remained healed all those years.

In some cases, people have insisted that their doctors remove the metal through surgery, and they are still doing well even after the skeptical doctors did what they were asked and paid to do. Don't take it the wrong way when I say "skeptical doctors," because I too believe in doctors. In fact, I have a dentist, a medical doctor, and even a chiropractor. If this surprises you, it should not, as Jesus had a doctor on His staff too, whose name was Luke. You know, of course, that Luke wrote two books in the Bible, including obviously the book of Luke and also the book of Acts. In fact, Paul often took Luke with him on the many recorded trips in the book of Acts, and I add that Paul took Dr. Luke with him because Paul was always getting beat up. My personal doctor has at times asked me to pray for him when he was in need of healing prayer. And He writes prescriptions for me as needed. I believe in healing, and it can come in a variety of God-given ways.

One of my personal medical testimonies is that I had skin cancer on my right ear for several years, and it got worse and worse and finally, after a trip to a dermatology specialist, I was told that portions of my ear would have to be surgically removed and that there would be at least four follow-up and reconstructive surgeries to reshape the ear. I was informed that this would cost around $150,000 to $200,000. Of course, I went to prayer and inquired of the Lord, and he told me to use a certain prescription cream and that would take care of the problem. So I went back to the specialist to ask for this cream, and he said that the cream works on flat surfaces, but not on intricate parts like an ear. I reinforced my request to use the cream by dispensing some healing testimonies and by sharing my belief that I had heard from God, but he reverted back to his medical knowledge. I kept insisting in a calm but firm way, asking if we could try it, as I would need his authorization to get the prescription written. He agreed to write it, but he said I would be back in a month or so for the surgery. Well, I was back in a month but never had to have the surgery, as God came through for me. Praise the Lord, as it only cost $20 for the cream rather than possibly $200,000 for a series of surgeries. I want you to understand that, in this case, the healing came through medicine and a direct word of knowledge from the Lord too.

In Acts 28:15 we are told that Paul took courage. I see many believers praying for courage and for boldness, but in most of the passages in the Bible that speak of these traits, the people are just told to walk in them or to rise up in that capacity. Joshua is told by God to be strong and courageous and then to be very strong and very courageous. The word *capacity* means to hold and contain, but it also means to release. A reservoir holds water but it also releases the water to the people to be used in their homes and places of employment. A fire station holds firefighting equipment, but if the station's capacity is only used to contain and not release the first responders with their trucks, the house will most likely burn down. An airport's capacity is to hold and utilize those things related to flying, but unless you are making a movie with Tom Hanks acting as a man stuck in an airport for an extended period of time, the airport's primary function with its capacity is to get people moving to their destinations.

Here is a story dealing with some of those first responders I just mentioned. Last August, I went to do some errands and came home to discover that my wife Diane had offered prayer for one of our neighbors. Here in Bellevue, there is an annual parade called "From Arrows to Aerospace," and our neighbors across the street had entered the parade driving an antique car. They also had another couple riding in the back of the car. When they arrived home after the parade, the man got out of the car and thought he had put the car in park. But he had actually left it in reverse, and as he was getting out, the car rolled backwards and knocked him to the ground.

Diane was outside in our yard at the time and saw this happen, as did several other neighbors. She went over to see if she could help. The car actually rolled down his driveway and up and over the curb at another neighbor's house. The man picked himself up, walked over to the car, got in it, put it in park, and then collapsed unconscious, with his body now slumped over the door.

At this point, more neighbors had arrived, and some were talking about what to do, including calling the EMS to come and assist. Diane put her hand on the man's shoulder and simply prayed for him to be well, and suddenly he woke up. The EMS arrived shortly later with other emergency vehicles. When he was medically examined, it was determined that nothing was wrong, and he did not need to be transported to the hospital.

These are the types of power encounters, or Kingdom Encounters, that also make a difference in the lives of others as we access God's supernatural provision for any circumstance that is set before us. God wants to use us to help others through our prayers. Over 20 years ago, when I was sick with an incurable disease and pain was my number one symptom, I would sometimes wake myself up at night crying, and Diane would gently pray in the spirit until I fell back asleep.

This is the kind of virtuous wife that Proverbs 31 speaks about. The Bible is correct when it says that he who finds a wife finds a good thing (Prov. 18:22). But finding a peaceful, kind, and gentle wife who is prayer-filled and an anointed, virtuous woman is like marrying into a perpetual Kingdom Encounter. This is because of the anointing that she carries due to the glory that is arising in her life. Diane is full of the Holy Spirit, but she does not just retain His presence—she pours out the presence of God through the anointing in so many wonderful ways.

We also hold the Holy Spirit and are supposed to be filled with His presence, but if we only contain the Holy Spirit and never release Him to do the work of the ministry and back up our actions with His power, then we are certainly not doing what God asks us to do, nor are we very courageous, as the Holy Spirit give us courage too. We discover the Holy Spirit's connection to courage in the Amplified Bible's rendition of Acts 4:31: "And when they had prayed, the place in which they were assembled was shaken; and they were all filled with the Holy Spirit, and they continued to speak the Word of God with freedom and boldness and courage."

And as I read this verse just now I saw the aspect of continuing. This is critical to so many believers who start something but never or rarely finish. We need to finish strong. Jesus said that He came to finish the work of His Father. Jesus was also a carpenter, so that word *finish* can have another definition relating to polish and shining as well. In Numbers 6:25, we see a prayer asking for God to shine His face upon us. What a glorious conclusion! What a glorious connection! What a glorious instruction! Maybe I can summarize it this way with the words, "Wow! Wow! Wow!"

As a family, we decided we would take some courage and host a worldwide healing prayer service on Facebook. So we started announcing it a few days in advance so that our friends could let their friends know. We selected worship music on Spotify and encouraged those who participated to listen to our worship song selections. That way, everyone who participated was engaged with the same music at the same time.

We set a date and decided to host this event for one hour. I had also invited some trustworthy friends to be available on my page to pray for people as well. As the service began, some people posted their prayer requests on my page, and my friends prayed for them. Others posted to me privately, and Jason and I had two laptop computers at our kitchen table, giving us both access to these private notes. We would read them, then type a prayer, then read the prayer out loud, then lay our hands on the computers and hit send. My wife Diane recorded everyone's name, location, and prayer need. We had people contacting us from places all over the world such as Turkey, Saudi Arabia, Peru, Columbia, Iceland, Canada, France, and many other countries as well.

Then, during the course of the next week, I received many emails and messages from people, including some we had never met who shared that, when we prayed for their conditions, the improvements began. In several cases, total healing was completed, and when it was all said and done, I believe we had sixty-five people who experienced significant or total healing. All this happened because we took a chance, or should I say, we took courage and stepped out in faith to see what God might do. It was amazing! Everyone had an encounter with God, including all my friends who were praying for others. It was wonderful.

At the church we attend, Eagle's Nest Worship Center in Omaha, Nebraska, there are so many testimonies of healing, powerful manifestations, and major breakthroughs. Here is one personally written by a friend documenting his Kingdom encounter from his perspective:

> My name is Channing Bunch, a covenant member at Eagle's Nest Worship Center in Omaha, Nebraska. I met Pastor West during a powerful worship experience at Eagle's Nest. At the time of the meeting, I had only been at Eagle's Nest a little under a year—and it was the first time I felt the outpouring of the Holy Spirit during a church service. I recall myself worshipping and praising God and feeling free to do so.
>
> Our Pastor, James Hart, asked Pastor West to come and assist in praying, prophesying, and laying hands

on the congregation. While I was in my zone of worship, Pastor West came to me and asked a few questions. I didn't know who Pastor West was, as there had not been any prior relationship between us.

The first question he asked was, "Have you been in a Musical Production before?"

My answer was, "Yes."

His second question was, "Do you play an instrument?"

I said, "Yes?"

Then came the challenging question. Pastor West asked, "If I tell you to go on stage and play the bongos, will you?"

I struggled with my answer, because here I am new to this ministry, the power of the Holy Spirit is flowing, Pastor Hart the Sunday before preached a message outlining the qualifications of Eagle's Nest Ministry, and this man I didn't even know wants me to go on stage and carry out this request. I eventually said yes because it showed obedience to the man of God and the fact that he was operating in the Spirit, because this man knew nothing about me.

WOW! WOW! WOW!

To validate his anointing, let me tell you, I was the leading actor in 1979 in a musical called "Bonds of Love," taken from the Hosea and Gomer relationship in the Book of Hosea. I also played the drums for two albums and many concerts for choirs across the city for over twenty years. What a truly awesome and anointed man of God.

Here are a couple more stories from Eagle's Nest. One lady who is our friend was coming to church high on drugs, but when that wore off, she would go in the bathroom and shoot up with the drug of her choice. However, during one of those episodes, she was delivered and set free from the bondage of addiction. She now heads up our ministry to the poor and needy. Another lady we know came to church drunk, but in the service, God supernaturally sobered her up, and she committed her life to Jesus and has been walking with Him ever since. Still another young man came to church with a loaded gun and an extra clip, but he encountered Jesus, laid down his weapon on the altar, walked away from it, and now walks with Jesus. Someone better be shouting *hallelujah* about now! Wow!

Sometimes, the people have an encounter even when they are not awake, as I have on more than one occasion been asked by local pastors to go to the hospital and pray for people who were on respirators and in a coma. In these cases, the people woke up the very next day. In one case, I got to speak to the attending physician, and he told me that in all of his years of medicine, he had never seen anyone wake up that fast from that type of coma before. He was actually startled and amazed! Now that is the encountering God I serve, for sure.

At another church, I was invited to speak and minister to children and teach them about the power of the Holy Spirit. This was with children in kindergarten through fifth grade. I taught about words of knowledge, what it means to fall under the power of God, and what can happen when you do. So I started praying for children around the room, and at one point we had 107 children laid out on the floor at the same time. As they began to get up, I then trained some of them to pray for others, and they also saw these and other manifestations.

In one case, I had a group of children stand about twenty feet away from me. Then I whispered to a group of children near me that I was going to say the colors of the rainbow, and when I got to the color blue, those children across the room, who did not hear anything I was saying, would suddenly fall over under the power of God. So I started slowly saying the colors red, orange, yellow, green, blue, and before I could say purple, that whole group standing across the room were no longer standing. They had fallen gently to the floor, with adult catchers positioned behind them to help them.

Another time, I was in Modesto, California, at a local church, and Jason and I were ministering to a bunch of youth and students mostly in high school. A bunch of guys came in riding their skateboards to church, and they had their boards lined up at the back of the worship center. I gave my message, and seventeen of them got saved that night. Then I began to pray, and many were falling under the power of the Lord. One girl was the pastor's daughter, and she came up healed from a kidney infection that had been causing her lots of pain. She also came up praying in the Spirit for the very first time.

But there was a group of really big guys who looked like football players, and they were standing off to the side. I asked them if they wanted a part of this too, and they kind of shrugged and said, "Okay." While standing about twelve to fifteen feet away, I simply asked the Holy Spirit to fall on them, and all of them crumpled to the floor. Later, they were asking their friends about how I was able to run over to them, push them all down, and then run back to where I was standing as if nothing had happened.

WOW! WOW! WOW!

All of their friends insisted that I never moved and I never touched them, which meant I could not possibly have pushed them either. This was a huge God thing for them. Then they too had some anointed afterglow (see chapter four), as there was a party planned after this service in the gym with lots of food, but no one wanted to leave. You know it is real when teenagers don't want to go eat but would rather stay in the presence of the Lord!

One of my favorite stories is that of an encounter in Target one morning. I went through the line, where a nice Black lady was waiting on the customers, scanning the items. When she was finished scanning my stuff, she had to take my credit card and run it through on her side, as the little machine was not working on my side. She tried several times, but it would not work, so I volunteered to try. She agreed, and it worked immediately. She smiled and said I must have the Midas touch. I agreed, but then I added, "I think I have the Target touch." Then I took courage and said, "You know what? I think I have the God touch."

At this point she smiled real big and said, "Yes, I think you do have the God touch." She then asked if I was a believer, and I said I was. I asked if she was a believer, and she said she was. At that moment, she raised her hand to give me a high five, so I did the same; and just after our hands met in the air, she spun around on her side of the register. I did not want to be outdone, so I spun around on my side of the counter as well. As this happened, everyone in our aisle quickly backed their carts out and left. It was rather humorous, but it was also a God moment.

We then shared about her church and my church, talked about God, and even quoted a couple of Bible passages. She told me that when she came in that day, her boss chewed her out for something she did not do wrong but was actually someone else's mistake. Because of this, she came to her post with a negative attitude, complaining about how bad the day was going to be. And then I came through her line, and she said, "Now I can make it." This was a God encounter that only cost me time, but the testimony has been shared many times and inspired others to reach out and be a blessing to business employees too.

I sometimes pay for gas, groceries, or coffee for others, even in drive-through lines where they can't even thank me. This also includes toll roads and parking lots like the ones at the airport. Every time I do it, I check to be sure God is in it—usually just a quick prayer of confirmation. Jesus said He only did what He saw the Father doing, and that is the premise that I also follow. But when He is involved, there are so many wonderful things that happen, and often others are touched in the process. This creates more ministry and more opportunities to share the gospel, pray for someone, or just minister peace and joy to those who need it that day.

My life is filled with stories about how God has worked in and through me to bless and encourage others. Of course, many of these stories are in my other books and on my blog for you to read at another time. There is information on the product page at the back of the book about these options.

I have seen so much and learned so much, yet there are countless numbers of other stories that could be written. I believe it is similar to Jesus, where the Bible says that volumes could have been written about his ministry. I am not comparing myself to Jesus, other than to say there is a whole lot more material that can be written, especially in this chapter. But I have whet your appetite and hopefully challenged you to believe for more.

As I stated earlier in the book, trust is a must. But as we trust God, it's like He opens a financial trust fund for us, and I am always blessed more than what I gave out. There has never been an exception to this. God comes through with larger gifts, better blessings, and really incredible responses to me when I step out in faith and courage to do what He is asking me to do at that moment. I have a message called "Moving from Moments to Momentum," and I literally walk and often am running in the momentum that

WOW! WOW! WOW!

God has me flowing in. But, as I wrote before too, there is no momentum in a swamp. We must avail ourselves to His river and the cascading effect of His rapids, sometimes slow and other times with a quick pace. We must be ready in season and out. It is imperative for the advancement of the Kingdom that our response time is prompt when He is calling and asking us to step in a make a difference. The rewards will amaze you, and the testimonies will influence you to the point where all you may be able to say after, "Praise the Lord," is, "Wow, Wow, Wow!"

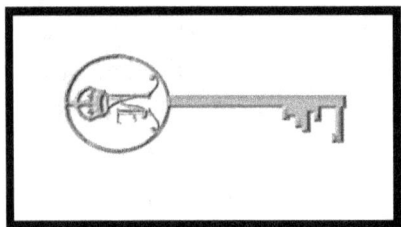

Kingdom Key # 7: Get ready!

In the old childhood game of hide and seek, the one who would begin seeking would call out and let the others know he was coming with these words: "Ready or not, here I come!"

There is an urgency in the Kingdom today for God to use us to reach as many as possible because, while He has tarried on coming again, His return is much sooner now than it was years ago. While that second coming will be glorious beyond description, He is also here now with His real presence to make a difference in your life and the lives of others. Jesus has some wows to show you and me that we have never seen before, and I believe that they are so incredible that it will make us respond by saying the word backwards: "Wow!"

I am serious! It is like a double-wow that takes our breath away when we experience God working in and through us like we have only previously read about in the lives of others. Let me encourage you this day to ask God for some wow moments. Then, take the courage and step out in what He is asking you to do. I could give you a list of possibilities, but according to Ephesians 3:20, He is able to do exceedingly more than we could possibly think or say. In other words, I could make a list for you from now until next year at this time, but God could easily select something beyond that list and ask you to do it, and it would be a perfect fit for you and the person you are reaching out to assist.

WOW! WOW! WOW!

So my encouragement is this: Get ready! Position yourself in a stance of readiness that defines who you are as a follower and disciple of Jesus. This will enable you to be able to respond at a moment's notice, perhaps at Target, at your church, at your job, on your block, or even at the airport or on a flight to your destination. Unlike the movie *Mission: Impossible*, in reality, this truth is, "Mission: Possible!" Your instructions, should you choose to respond to them, will undoubtedly open up new avenues of wonderful Kingdom adventures and Kingdom Encounters that will keep you talking about them for a long time. Will you take the initiative? Will you respond to the challenge? Will you follow Jesus a little more boldly today than you have in the past?

Lord Jesus, bless the person who is reading this book right now with new courage, boldness, and tenacity to reach out and step out in faith this week with energy that is from You and with anointing that is from You. Help them to carry out Your assigned task and see You work through them in ways that they previously thought were not possible. Thank you Jesus for helping them expand Your Kingdom. I am grateful that they are growing in their faith and will soon have some incredible testimonies to share because they trusted in you. Thank you, Jesus. Amen!

Chapter Eight
Prepare for the Arrival of Revival

Back in the mid-90s, when I was a pastor in rural Kansas, I took the majority of our church members to visit and experience the Pensacola Revival in Pensacola, Florida. Our son Jason was five years old at the time and was traveling with us. We drove in several cars from southwest Kansas to Oklahoma City, where we caught our plane to Pensacola. Of course, on the plane, there was the normal protocol of preflight announcements, along with a few more before landing.

We discovered that there were a number of other people on our flight who were also flying to Pensacola to attend the revival just like our group was, so we had some interaction with these folks, and it was a great time of visiting and anticipation. Some of them had previously been there like I had, while others were going there for the very first time, such as Steve and Cindy Hittle, who are mentioned on the dedication page.

At one point, the pilot came on the speaker and told all of us to prepare for arrival. But Jason thought he said to everyone on the plane, "Prepare for revival." That one situation has long since been a wonderful reminder to all of us that God wants us to experience revival in an ongoing way. And through the ministry of the International House of Prayer in Kansas City, along with Randy Clark in Pennsylvania and Bill Johnson in Redding, California, we have learned and now appreciate that revival is not an event, but rather a lifestyle and an ongoing Kingdom experience. In reality, it is a culture that needs to be cultivated. As

Bill Johnson has been known to say, much of the church in America revolves around a sermon, but instead it should be revolving around God's presence. It's His presence that makes a difference.

We now understand we can encounter God in so many ways and in so many situations that just affirm to us and those around us that the Kingdom of God is within us and is breaking in around us, as I have already taught and shared in previous chapters. Now that you are more than halfway through this book, I want to begin encouraging you to prepare for the arrival of revival in your own life.

I've had some people tell me that in order to have revival, you have to have vival. Not all words with "re" in front of them as a prefix also have a root word that can stand alone in definition and understanding. Some words truly only make sense with that "re" prefix in front. For instance referee, reference, and refrain are among many such words. For me, the basic understanding of revival is to encounter and experience the life of God in a fresh and perhaps even new way that extends His presence into our lives. This encounter often ends up promoting godliness, vision, and a strong desire just to hang out with God rather than anything else that we normally would enjoy doing. Having a theophany that Jason wrote about in the introduction demonstrates that the experience is an option worth pursuing. So many people either talk about what happened years ago without having ongoing experiences and theophanies today, or they elaborate about an elusive future experience based on their desire to see something happen, but they have their lists of preceding events that must happen first.

I've known people who said, "When I get enough money," or, "When I get enough teaching," or, "When I get enough others to agree with me, then I will step out." But God says, "Go." He doesn't qualify that "Go" with, "Wait for these other provisions before you go." Just go! Sometimes, our going includes bringing people to the point of coming into His presence too. So we have coming and going with theophany and experiences in both realms. In John 10:9 we read that Jesus is the door or the gate, and as we go in and out we find pasture. In other words, regardless of the direction we are going, whether in or out, we discover feeding, anointing, provision, and opportunities to experience Jesus. It's as if the door is painted, and each time we proceed through the doorway, we get some wet paint on our sleeve.

I already shared in a previous chapter about how the anointed afterglow often keeps people from wanting to leave church so quickly, not recognizing that it was the anointing that was so attractive to them. Yet they could not find a good reason to leave because of the very presence of God in the room.

One similar story happened to me several years ago at a Vineyard Fellowship in California where I was invited to speak and minister. The senior pastor had asked me to try to keep the service to ninety minutes, but no one consulted the Lord about that time request. At one point, the praise band led in the initial worship set the Hillsong arrangement of "Shout unto God." After my message, I felt led to have the people come forward and sing that song again from the front of the worship center, with the praise band leading it. What happened was that the nearly 150 people who flooded the front literally out sang the band, who had microphones and amplification for their instruments. Somehow, the people in their enthusiasm sang and sang that one song over and over for thirty plus minutes. This, in turn, launched several hours of ministry and worship, and when it was all said and done, the service had lasted five and a half hours, starting at 6:00 p.m. and concluding around 11:30 p.m.

At that point, there were still about thirty people in the building, and some began to ask if it was possible to do that again the next night. I was scheduled to fly home the next day, but the leaders met, and I was invited to stay an additional night. We all recognized that it would be a Monday night, which in reality is one of the toughest nights, if not the toughest night, to get people to come to a church meeting. There was a reason that the Pensacola revival did not meet on Monday evenings during its historic seven-year run.

These people in California were excited, and they began to contact those who had already left and encourage their friends to return. Would you believe it, on a Monday evening, people from all over Los Angeles showed up to encounter the presence of God! I met some people who drove sixty miles one way to attend. We had over 300 in attendance too. They had come out to have a theophany and get some wet paint on their sleeves. There was such a hunger and a desire for a fresh new move of God that many people just laid aside their own schedules, even at the beginning of a new work week, to come out and see what God was doing.

I remember another similar scenario at a smaller church, also a Vineyard, down in Louisiana where I was invited to come and speak on a Saturday night and a Sunday morning to a group that averaged thirty-five in attendance. I told the pastor in advance that if anything like revival started or opened up, I could rearrange my schedule and stay a few extra nights. As it turned out, I ended up staying twelve nights, and that little church tripled in size from 35 to 105 people in just twelve days. Isn't that amazing? The people would leave the services each night and go witness at Wal-Mart, Shoney's, and Waffle House, sometimes staying up to 3:00 a.m. just talking to others about Jesus and inviting them to return to this revival. Many came, got right with God, were healed of illnesses, and began to have a new journey with Jesus, all because a local pastor was willing to take a chance and prepare for the arrival of revival.

I am wondering what you are already dreaming about for your church. I bet many who are reading this right now are getting downloads from heaven that are inspiring dreams and visions for what could take place at their own local and home church. I think I should stop momentarily and pray for a special heavenly download for you now.

> Jesus, I ask that those who are reading this book and chapter right now would indeed receive a special imparted message from you, a dream or a vision, an insight and a passion, that would stimulate a revival atmosphere in their personal lives and church. I pray that You, Lord, would send them something significant that demonstrates Your power and Your authority to perceive, receive, believe and achieve something greater than themselves. I am asking that this will change the spiritual climate around them, wherever they walk and gather, so that their measure of rule and spheres of influence will expand heavenly realms of power, grace, and revival in those specific areas. Thank You, Jesus, that Your influence is inclusive of everyone who is seeking You. I believe right now that Kingdom expansion is flowing to those reading this prayer to target a new area of the life flowing river of God in their lives today. Thank You so much, Father. Amen!

As previously stated, I am learning that revival is not so much an event, but rather a lifestyle. Thus, with each day, I experience revival in various ways, whether praying for a stranger in the marketplace, witnessing on Facebook, writing incredible testimonies on my blog, preaching a message in a church, praying over and with business leaders and politicians, or simply reading my Bible at home, I am having Kingdom encounters that have a revival taste to them with every bite. The Bible says to taste and see that the Lord is good. And His goodness and mercy are new every morning, thus providing new opportunities for me to experience new tastes and sights each and every day. This can be true for you too.

Bill Johnson, in his book *Strengthen Yourself in the Lord*,[12] writes, "If I don't stay aware of the God who invades the impossible, I will reduce ministry to my ministry gifts. All of our gifts are like the sails on a boat. We can sit in the harbor (church) and admire one another's sails; but without wind they are worthless! Our gifts are designed to watch the wind of God so we can accomplish what is humanly impossible. The testimony keeps our sails hoisted."

We have a saying here in Omaha: When the tide comes in, all the boats rise at the same time. As ministry leaders in the city, we want to experience God and His Kingdom, and it is critical that we try to do what we see our Father doing here in Omaha, just as Jesus declared in John 5:19 that He only did what He saw the Father doing too. We have many stories of pastors and churches blessing other pastors and churches.

It is imperative that we keep our eyes open to what God is doing, rather than what men are doing or what we have previously seen men do. Many in the church today are so drawn into success that they try to follow the methods of others that brought them success, not realizing that God often leads one person one way and another person in a different direction, especially when leading a ministry, church, or a team of disciples. My examples in this chapter and others are not meant to be methodologies of how to experience God, but rather stimulants to show you that God can be experienced in a variety of ways. My intent is not to limit your theophany to merely attending church, being involved in a prayer group, or participating in a home group.

Bill Johnson wrote about not admiring one another's sails, and that is a good word. We like to be admired for what we have or have accomplished, but with the gifts of the Spirit, and any anointing that we might possess, all of the admiration needs to go and flow toward Jesus. If we are to watch anything, we must watch the wind of God and then simply join in the direction that He is flowing and blowing! It really is simple, yet so strategic. So often, churchgoing people try to make it difficult by trying to work something up, praying hard and loud enough, singing long and clapping enthusiastically, but as with Elijah in 1 Kings 19:11–13, what we think will attract God or where we position ourselves is not always the location that God will be found.

> Then He said, "Go out, and stand on the mountain before the LORD." And behold, the LORD passed by, and a great and strong wind tore into the mountains and broke the rocks in pieces before the LORD, but the LORD was not in the wind; and after the wind an earthquake, but the LORD was not in the earthquake; and after the earthquake a fire, but the LORD was not in the fire; and after the fire a still small voice.

> So it was, when Elijah heard it, that he wrapped his face in his mantle and went out and stood in the entrance of the cave.

Most of us are unwilling to go to the cave because we like action, motion, movement, noise, and activity. But the cave is a place of refuge and often a place of solace where God likes to speak. The cave is really just a place in nature where things are quiet. It can be on a mountaintop, in a meadow, up in a tree house, on a park bench, or in a tent in the middle of the forest. It's been said of Jesus that He went from one prayer meeting to another and performed ministry in-between. To be about the Father's business meant that Jesus had to have alone times to learn directly from the CEO of the family business. This warranted times away from the crowds and the masses. But church folks today seem to do just the opposite and try to discover what God is doing in larger group settings, avoiding the more intimate times with Jesus for more glamorous public and modernized church life that includes multiple media networks and connections. Jason will write more about this in chapter nine.

When King David returned to Ziklag and found that his whole town had burned to the ground and all of his family and the families of all of his men had been kidnapped and taken to another land and place, he discovered that he was between a rock and a hard place, in that his men were disowning him and spoke of stoning him. Everything that was stable in David's life was now becoming unstable, but the one sure thing that he knew he could rely on was an encounter with God. So we learn in 1 Samuel 3 that when David found a place and prayed, he received the word of the Lord to make a leader's decision and then go after the crooks, robbers, and kidnappers with the intention of recovering everything. And that is exactly what God delivered into his hands: everything! But David had to get alone with God to discover God's next step in the journey.

In the New Testament, it is my understanding that Jesus prayed for and healed six different blind guys six different ways. It would have been easy to follow a method, but in each case, God was doing it differently, so Jesus had to adapt to the new strategy and plan. There are occasions when praying for the sick or someone with a need, that a previous method or way will pop into my head while praying, and I will ask God if that is what He wants to do and then proceed based on what I hear. Often, I get a fresh and brand new word for everyone I am praying for, and if you hang around me long enough, you will hear me say something like this: "I have never prayed or done this before." This is new territory, with new strategies and new guidelines, so I just try to flow with what God is doing at that moment. I work very hard at making sure I don't fall into the same trap that Jesus spoke against in Mark 7:13, where the traditions of men could make the Word of God lose its effect. I never want to lose my Kingdom effectiveness, so I must stay focused on what the Lord is doing and saying.

Ephesians 3:7 in the Amplified Bible really adds needed understanding and clarification with these words, "Of this [Gospel] I was made a minister according to the gift of God's free grace (undeserved favor) which was bestowed on me by the exercise (the working in all its effectiveness) of His power."

Notice the effectiveness of His power. If I come up with an idea of how to minister, then it is my power that is working to bring a solution, resolution, or answer. But if it is God's power, then the effectiveness is never questioned. It is based on righteousness, and the people rejoice. It flows from a heavenly realm, and the results are always promoting and projecting a positive Kingdom-oriented answer and result that can't be thwarted, undone, or discontinued. The sent word of God in Isaiah 55:11 contains these promises: "So shall My word be that goes forth from My mouth; It shall not return to Me void, But it shall accomplish what I please, And it shall prosper in the thing for which I sent it."

Genesis 1:1–2 states, "In the beginning God created the heavens and the earth. The earth was without form, and void; and darkness was on the face of the deep. And the Spirit of God was hovering over the face of the waters." In verse 3 when God spoke, the void on earth from verse 2 ended and became un-voided, as God's Word from Isaiah 55 stated that it will not return void. The void was then replaced with God's spoken Word of creation.

God intends for those who respond to His Word to prosper and to see life appear in a voided area where death was previously knocking. I envision that God wants our spiritual vital statistics to radically improve as we encounter Him at various levels.

The word *encounter* is broken up in English like this: "en" is a prefix forming verbs that have the general sense "to cause (a person or thing) to be in" the place, condition, or state named by the stem; and the first definition of the root word "counter" is one that is an opposite.[13][14] By *opposite*, I mean something like a counterattack or a counteroffer. So if we combine these two definitions of this word, we discover that we are to be in the place, condition, and state of God, Who is the opposite of us, but Who has worked tirelessly to place Himself in a position so that there is an exchange through the encounter and we have the opportunity to have His characteristics, traits, and power permanently downloaded to us.

We need to prepare for this encountering revival to have a definite lasting change in our lives that so radically affects us that we never want to go back to our old life. The chorus and the verse to the song *I Need You More*, by Lindell Cooley, lends itself to this process of encountering revival.[15]

> I need You more,
> More than yesterday.
> I need You, Lord,
> More than words can say.
> I need You more
> Than ever before.
> I need You, Lord.
> I need You, Lord.
>
> More than the air I breathe;
> More than the song I sing;
> More than the next heartbeat;
> More than anything.
>
> And Lord as time goes by,
> I'll be by Your side,
> 'Cause I never want to go back to my old life.

Obviously, most of us would rather not return to an old life that has elements of evil, corrupt habits, addictions, and other ungodly lifestyles, but often these past histories enable the enemy to get a foothold due to something we call shame. Shame has a way of holding us back from going forward with the Lord in what He has planned for our lives. There is an older chorus that was popular for many years in the church called "Trading My Sorrows."[16] Part of the song lyrics stated that we are trading our sorrows, trading our pain, trading our sickness, and trading our shame. But of the four things mentioned that are to be traded away, shame seems to be the hardest one for the believers to trade.

This is part of the theme of chapter four, where I briefly addressed the difference between a swamp and a river. People will use the blame game to move you into the shame game and live with them in the swamp. In the swamp, all the animals devour one another, and shame, when manifesting in someone else, often sets others on edge against us. They then use defensive weapons of control, verbal abuse, and disqualification to try to get us and others to live where they live, in the swamp, rather than in the river of God. This is often used as a substitute or excuse for why the power of God can't be utilized. I believe this is a possible answer to why no previous pastor or professor told me about the power of the Holy Spirit that I wrote about in chapter one. Some leaders actually appear to be ashamed of the gospel of Christ, even though Romans 1:16 states otherwise.

We access the power of the gospel in Romans 1:16, and we receive the power of the Holy Spirit in Acts 1:8. Because some only have a form of godliness but deny the power, as shared in 2 Timothy 3, the results are a powerless church with form and ritual but few Kingdom Encounters. I actually met an assistant pastor at a church I was ministering at on the east coast who confided in me that he did not believe in the Bible or the power of God. He was filling in for the senior pastor, who had another commitment during that service. He then went on to tell me that he could lead the worship service like doing any other job because he was paid to do so. I still had an amazing weekend of ministry because God is not limited by one person's lack of faith.

Let's read a couple of familiar passages in the Bible to see how and where shame is listed and examined. Look at the famous passage that is often quoted from Joel 2:28, which reads like this: "And it shall come to pass afterward that I will pour out My Spirit on all flesh; Your sons and your daughters shall prophesy, Your old men shall dream dreams, Your young men shall see visions." Right before this verse comes these words from verses 25–27:

> So I will restore to you the years that the swarming locust has eaten, the crawling locust, the consuming locust, and the chewing locust, My great army which I sent among you. You shall eat in plenty and be satisfied, and praise the name of the LORD your God, Who has dealt wondrously with you; and My people shall never be put to shame. Then you shall know that I am in the midst of Israel: I am the LORD your God and there is no other. My people shall never be put to shame.

Verse 25 is a vivid picture of what happens when shame is coming upon you, as it feels like others are eating you alive just with their looks of disdain and eyes filled with accusation. But God says it twice that His people will not be put to shame. When God says something twice, you know it is important.

Now take a look at Romans 10:8–11:

> But what does it say? 'The word is near you, in your mouth and in your heart' (that is, the word of faith which we preach): that if you confess with your

> mouth the Lord Jesus and believe in your heart that God has raised Him from the dead, you will be saved. For with the heart one believes unto righteousness, and with the mouth confession is made unto salvation. For the Scripture says, 'Whoever believes on Him will not be put to shame.'

The word of God is near you and in your mouth and in your heart, and it does not include any place or have any room for shame to be a part of the furniture that is displayed in the room. Romans 8:14–15 declares:

> How then shall they call on Him in whom they have not believed? And how shall they believe in Him of whom they have not heard? And how shall they hear without a preacher? And how shall they preach unless they are sent? As it is written: "How beautiful are the feet of those who preach the gospel of peace, who bring glad tidings of good things!"

There is nothing pretty about shame at all. It is removed with and by the power of Jesus through repentance and forgiveness and is not expected to have a place to reside in our lives.

Second Corinthians 4:2 enhances our stance with these words: "But we have renounced the hidden things of shame, not walking in craftiness nor handling the word of God deceitfully, but by manifestation of the truth commending ourselves to every man's conscience in the sight of God." We are to avoid the manifestation of shame and blame, and walk in newness of life and His righteousness to avoid being sucked under in a spiritual undertow or rip current that is trying to rip away the anointing and power of God from our lives because of a previous deed, act, or sin that has long been forgiven and buried in the depth of the sea with the rest of our sins. It is important to proclaim what the Word of God says about us, not what our circumstances say, what others declare, or even what our shameful feelings may be dealing us.

By doing this, we maintain a state of readiness for revival and the arrival of the presence of Jesus in our lives for the work of the ministry including any daily tasks that He may call us to do today. I know in my life I have said things, watched things, looked at things, retold things, and often acted unrighteous. If left undone without repentance and forgiveness, the shame, which is a sham of the devil, would grow, fester, and greatly enlarge itself to unhealthy proportions that, like a fungus or a wart, can cause great harm. Then, condemnation sets in. But we must remind ourselves of the Bible's promise that there is no condemnation for those who are in Christ Jesus (Rom. 8:1).

James 5:16 declares, "Confess your trespasses to one another, and pray for one another, that you may be healed. The effective, fervent prayer of a righteous man avails much." There's that word *effective* again, changing a heart and manifesting grace to yourself and then to others as you appropriate forgiveness and freedom. This, in turn, will set you up to be able to prepare for the arrival of revival, an ongoing culture that will change your daily life from routine to supernatural and exciting as you live in such a way that enables the power of the Holy Spirit to be released in your life every single day.

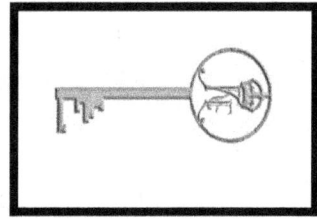

Kingdom Key #8: Bring shalom to the sham of shame.

Look at Psalm 18:23 in the Voice, which reads, "I was blameless before Him; I kept myself from guilt *and shame*." It's up to God to deliver you from shame, but it's up to you to keep yourself from shame. You must not let the enemy or others convince you that your past dictates your future; otherwise, you will never experience true levels of intense revival, and at the conclusion of your life, you will wonder what could have been. In the NASB, Psalm 34:5 says, "They looked to Him and were radiant, and their faces will never be ashamed."

Let's briefly read these words of Paul in Philippians 3:12–15:

> Not that I have already attained, or am already perfected; but I press on, that I may lay hold of that for which Christ Jesus has also laid hold of me. Brethren, I do not count myself to have apprehended; but one thing I do, forgetting those things which are behind and reaching forward to those things which are ahead, I press toward the goal for the prize of the upward call of God in Christ Jesus.

Therefore let us, as many as are mature, have this mind; and if in anything you think otherwise, God will reveal even this to you.

A simple sign of being mature as a believer is not being engaged in looking back. Paul said that one thing he does, which, when you read, it sounds like two things, but in actuality this act is combined into two distinct motions simultaneously so that it appears as one thing. He says in verse 13 that this one thing combines forgetting the past and reaching forward. You must take the position that what is coming up with God is far more important than anything that has happened in your past. You must also realize that the next step with Jesus is what will fulfill your destiny and that nothing in your past can be changed or altered, but it can be forgotten and reissued to you as something brand new, useful, and incredibly anointed, without any lingering stain or defect.

You are free to pursue and explore God's Kingdom as a child of the King, Who wants to release and see the Kingdom flowing in, on, and around you in a continual outflow and manifestation that ushers you into a culture of revival. Get prepared now!

Finally, let the peace of God provide shalom for the sham of shame. As Pastor Ken Sinclair from Faith Lutheran Church in Sugar Land, Texas, used to declare, "Shame off you!"

Chapter Nine
Prayer Encounters
By Jason West

In this book, you have learned about Kingdom Encounters, which come in many forms and have many effects. Now, I have the privilege of wrapping everything up and bringing this book to a conclusion. I guess it's true: I really do love to have the last word!

The thought I want to leave you with is this: Kingdom Encounters must be founded on prayer encounters. To explain what I mean, let me first return to the verse I listed at the beginning of the introduction to this book. Matthew 6:10 states, "Your kingdom come. Your will be done on earth as it is in heaven." As I mentioned at the beginning, this is what a Kingdom Encounter is all about: God's Kingdom encountering the earth and His will being done on earth, just as it is in heaven. Yet, where is this imperative statement found? It is found in the Lord's Prayer.

Regarding Kingdom Encounters, the key is this: Kingdom Encounters flow out of the faithful, fervent, and expectant prayers of God's people. While God does encounter His people unexpectedly on multiple occasions, there is something to be said for an encounter which comes as a result of the people of God passionately pressing in for a breakthrough. There are many instances in the Bible in which people are instructed to pray and intercede for a specific cause until the breakthrough happens. In Isaiah 62:6–7, we see one such example: "I have set watchmen on your walls, O Jerusalem; they shall never hold their peace day or night. You who make mention of the LORD, do not keep silent, and give Him no rest till He establishes and till He makes Jerusalem a praise in the earth." The watchmen of the Lord were instructed to incessantly cry out to God on behalf of the people until they saw the fulfillment of what He promised. This is what it means to watch and pray, as Jesus told His disciples to do in Matthew 26:41. In order to elaborate on this, please allow me to share from my recent book *Who Will Ascend?* This excerpt is from the chapter entitled "Jesus' Mountaintop Experiences": [17]

> Let's now look at perhaps the most key mountaintop experience that Jesus had: His experience at the Mount of Olives. It was during this famous episode, found in Luke 22:39–46, that Jesus labored in prayer while His disciples slept nearby. His prayer was so laborious that He actually sweated drops of blood. During this time, Jesus gave an interesting directive for His disciples to follow. He said, "Pray that you may not enter into temptation" (Lk. 22:40). The passage in Matthew 26:41 adds another aspect to this: "Watch and pray, lest you enter into temptation." Not only were the disciples to pray, but they were to *watch* and pray.

> Jesus placed this mandate over His disciples, a mandate that simply meant for them to watch and pray. Yet, the disciples were so weary from the cares of life and the toils of the day that they could not stay awake. It was just too much. Jesus' heart was grieved when He returned to find them sleeping instead of keeping watch in prayer. "Could you not watch with Me one hour?" He cried (Matt. 26:40). He knew their cares were great. He knew their bodies were weak. In fact, He knew they deeply wanted to watch in prayer with Him, for He said,

"The spirit indeed is willing, but the flesh is weak" (Matt. 26:41). The fleshly desires of the disciples were a great source of weakness for them. How many of us are like that today? God is calling His people to a great level of intercession, but in order for us to intercede, we must lay down our burdens and cry out to God for strength that only He can give.

But the question remains: "What does it mean to watch and pray?" Well, the way I see it is that prayer is one level of communication between God and man. But watching and praying is another whole level: It is the level of intercession. Intercession is not just prayer; it is more than that! Pure, real, impacting intercession is the combination of watching and praying. To pray means to converse with God about any given topic or subject. To watch is to take responsibility for a certain people group in everything those people do. The combination, therefore, is the state of intercession. Watching is like performing the job of a biblical watchman.

In the times of ancient Israel, cities were surrounded by walls with entrances through gates *[such as the gate pictured on the cover of this book]*. Positioned at every gate was at least one watchman. His job was to keep guard over the city and to regulate who entered and exited the city. If a large army were to lay siege over the city, it was the ultimate responsibility of the watchman to relay that information to the leaders of the city. If he failed to get that information across and the army besieged and obliterated the city, the bloodshed of the innocent was ultimately on the watchman's head...

Two principles that we need to remember about watchmen are that they are relentless and restless. A good example of this is the Moravians from the days of old. Led by Count von Zinzendorf, the Moravians spearheaded a 100-year 24/7 prayer movement in which the prayers never ceased and the revival fires never went out. They were the watchmen of their day.[18] Today, similar prayer movements have sprung up in houses of prayer all across the nation of the United States and across the world. Oh, that we would live in the day of the watchmen. Oh, that we would stand among a people whose spirits are willing and who are strong to resist the temptation of their flesh so that they may continue in prayer and intercession!

The watchmen incessantly stood in the gap between the people in the city and the outsiders. Additionally, they took full responsibility for any harm that came upon the city if they did not forewarn the people. This is not unlike the instructions the Lord gave to Ezekiel in Ezekiel 3:17–19:

Son of man, I have made you a watchman for the house of Israel; therefore hear a word from My mouth, and give them warning from Me: When I say to the wicked, "You shall surely die," and you give him no warning, nor speak to warn the wicked from his wicked way, to save his life, that same wicked man shall die in his iniquity; but his blood I will require at your hand. Yet, if you warn the wicked, and he does not turn from his wickedness, nor from his wicked way, he shall die in his iniquity; but you have delivered your soul.

How does this practically look in society today? It certainly must take the form of listening to the Lord for His words of wisdom, and speaking those words to those around us. Watchmen are responsible to give any warnings that the Lord would utter, as well as any words of wisdom or counsel. Additionally, being a watchman means guarding the backs of the people, including other watchmen. We need to learn how to work with a trowel in one hand and a sword in the other, much like the people in Nehemiah's day. Let's read this biblical example from Nehemiah 4:7–9, 16–18 of what it means to be a watchman on a wall:

Now it happened, when [the enemies] heard that the walls of Jerusalem were being restored and the gaps were beginning to be closed, that they became very angry, and all of them conspired together to come and attack Jerusalem and create confusion. Nevertheless we made our prayer to our God, and because of them we set a watch against them day and night. . . . So it was, from that time on, that half of my servants worked at construction, while the other half held the spears, the shields, the bows, and wore armor; and the leaders were behind all the house of Judah. Those who built on the wall, and those who carried burdens, loaded themselves so that with one hand they worked at construction, and with the other held a weapon. Every one of the builders had his sword girded at his side as he built. And the one who sounded the trumpet was beside me.

Watching in prayer takes unity and teamwork. The disciples lacked this when they were on the mountain. Instead, I have to believe that they tried to stay awake by their own strength, rather than relying on each other for support. Being a watchman is not a job to be done alone. The Israelites in Nehemiah's day prevailed because they stood together and worked together to ward off their enemies. However, the disciples did not watch, and while they were sleeping, the "hour, and the power of darkness" crept in (Lk. 22:53).

Watch is a warfare term. We have to know that as we learn how to pray and intercede, we are involved in a great battle. Serious prayer and intercession stirs up the powers of darkness, but even more so, it stirs up the power of God. As we learn to watch and pray, we must learn to focus on God and His glory. When we do that, every weapon of the enemy becomes null and void, and his power is demolished. Remember, it is by watching and praying that we are able to resist temptation.

Indeed, Kingdom encounters come through the prayers of the saints: relentless, importunate prayers. When we pray, we need to believe that our prayers touch heaven and impact earth. The level of kingdom impact you have on earth is directly related to your prayer life. This is why God instructed us to *pray* for His kingdom to encounter this earth. He did not simply tell us to believe, hope, or wish for it; He told us to be directly involved in the process by praying for it. Prayers are not insignificant. It is easy for us to think our prayers are never heard or that they don't actually accomplish anything, but the Bible does not lie when it tells us, "The effective, fervent prayer of a righteous man avails much" (James 5:16). Prayers are effective and fervent when they are combined with relentless, watchful intercession.

We hear the above verse all the time, but do we believe it? Many times, the way we pray indicates that we don't. I am sure that the enemy loves it when we decide not to pray because we think it doesn't do any good. Every time the enemy convinces us not to pray, he experiences a glimpse of victory, while we experience a shadow of defeat. Of course, all the enemy's seeming victories come to complete ruin in the end. But still, why would we ever want to even give him a glimpse of victory?

You can experience the kingdom of God every day simply by taking the initiative to pray and spend that time with Him. Every time we pray, we experience a piece of God's Kingdom on earth. We have the amazing privilege to experience a Kingdom Encounter every time we pray! Why? Because, when we pray, God is in our midst to hear and answer our prayers. And when God is in our midst, He is Immanuel, "God with us." And as you know, when we experience Immanuel, we experience a continual theophany encounter with God.

In this sense, then, we can look at the next part of the Lord's Prayer in a new light. In Matthew 6:10–11, Jesus states, "Your kingdom come. Your will be done on earth as it is in heaven. Give us this day our daily bread." I have already written about the first part of this passage, but I wanted to include it again so you can see the context of the last sentence: "Give us this day our daily bread." Directly, I believe this verse indicates that we are to pray for God to provide for our daily needs. This is a widely accepted interpretation and one that I wholeheartedly support. However, in the context of God's Kingdom encountering the earth, I cannot help but wonder if this daily bread is somehow akin to this Kingdom Encounter.

Let me break it down. Jesus said to His disciples, "My food is to do the will of Him who sent Me, and to finish His work" (John 4:34). We are to model our lives after Jesus' example; therefore, our food (or bread) is to do the will of the Father and to finish His work. My dad wrote about this some in a previous chapter. We are to pray for His will to be done on earth as it is in heaven. How will this be accomplished? His will shall be done on earth as it is in heaven when heaven comes to earth. Heaven comes to earth when His Kingdom comes to earth. Essentially, what I am trying to communicate could be read as follows: "Your Kingdom come and encounter this earth. Your will be done on earth as it is in heaven. Give us this day our daily encounter."

What am I saying? I am saying that your daily encounter will flow out of your daily prayer life and your daily walk with Immanuel. Give us this day our daily encounter—our daily *Kingdom Encounter*. I believe that as we daily pray for God's Kingdom to come to earth and His will to be done on earth, He will follow that up by giving us daily encounters in His presence. It won't look the same every day, and some days you may not even recognize it at all, but truly, I believe that God wants to encounter us every day. For further elaboration on this, please read another excerpt from my book, taken from the section entitled "Time for a Testimony: Living on the Mountaintop":

> The more I learn about encounters, the more I am convinced that God desires us to experience Him in new ways every day. I can't live in yesterday's encounter, and I can't try to get by until tomorrow's

encounter. But I can live in the encounter God has for me today. In essence, as God's children, I believe God desires that we ascend on a daily basis, having daily encounters with Him. It is like manna, or "daily bread." He gives us what we need for each day.

How do we ascend and have mountaintop experiences on a daily basis? It all comes back to our prayer lives and the level of abandonment we have as we give ourselves to God. It comes back to the Psalm 24 lifestyle that God has called us to live. As we live this way, relying upon His strength, we will not have to live in the past or the future. Rather, we can say to God, "Give us this day our daily bread" (Matt. 6:11). Your daily mountaintop experience will flow out of your daily prayer life and your daily walk with God.

Thus, with all these things in mind, I make a simple appeal to you: Pray. When we pursue God for Kingdom Encounters but do not anchor our pursuit with a lifestyle of prayer, we easily lose focus and begin to rely on ourselves for the manifestation of these Kingdom Encounters. When we take prayer out of the equation, taking God out of the equation is not too far behind. And as you well know, that is a dangerous thing to do and a dangerous place to be.

Daily Kingdom Encounters flow out of daily prayer encounters. Do not ever fall into the fallacious belief that prayers do not accomplish anything. Prayer encounters lead to Kingdom Encounters—especially when those prayer encounters are fervent, importunate, and relentless. It's time to press in to what God has for us. Pressing in is not always easy—if it were easy, it would not be called *pressing* in. There is some sort of effort involved—some sort of initiative. I believe God honors this in a very real way and responds to it by encountering us in a very profound way. But it all begins with a simple prayer: "Your kingdom come. Your will be done on earth as it is in heaven. Give us this day our daily bread" (Matt. 6:10–11).

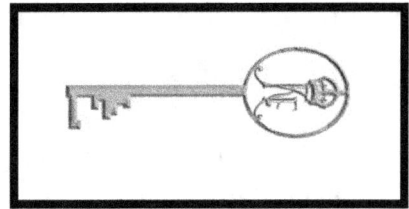

Kingdom Key #9: Without prayer, we can't prepare.

As you read in chapter 8, one of the things that believers who are hungry for Kingdom Encounters need to do is to prepare for revival. As we do this, we will find that prayer is a key ingredient that is necessary for assisting us in that preparation. Without prayer, we can't prepare. Prayer sets the foundation. Prayer sets the atmosphere.

With this in mind, knowing that you have reached the end of this book about Kingdom Encounters, stop and ask the Lord to show you how you should pray. There are certain things in your life and certain people in your sphere of influence that God has called you specifically to be a watchman for. We all have our own unique gaps that God has called us to stand in. Your gap looks different than my gap, but as watchmen and as intercessors, we all are called to stand in the gap on behalf of someone or something. Ask God right now, "What is my gap?" I believe He will reveal it to you when you ask Him. Perhaps you already know.

Once you know, then establish your post as a watchman in that gap. Do not fear if change does not happen overnight. Remember, watchmen are relentless and restless. But assuredly, if you do not lose your ground, if you keep pressing in, you *will* see revival. You *will* see breakthrough. Watchful prayer is the necessary ingredient for preparing for revival. I'll say it again: Without prayer, we can't prepare. The more you make prayer your foundation, the more you will begin to experience greater levels, greater frequency, and a greater intensity of Kingdom Encounters.

As you press in, I believe you will experience daily Kingdom Encounters that will at times leave you speechless and awestruck, with nothing left to say, but, "Wow! Wow! Wow! God did it again!" And guess what? As you continue to experience these Kingdom Encounters, you will continue to testify and glorify God. And as you continue to testify and glorify God, even more of His Kingdom will be released on earth, leading to more and more Kingdom Encounters. It just keeps spiraling upward from there. But it all starts with a person whose heart is willing to contend, to press in, and to passionately watch and pray on behalf of an individual, a church, a school, a city, and a nation. It starts with you.

Notes

1. West, Jason B. "Purposefulness." Web log post. *Chronicles of Prayer*. N.p., 22 Aug. 2013. Web. 22 Aug. 2013.

2. Bevere, John. *Driven by Eternity: Making Life Count Today and Forever*. New York: Warner Faith, 2006. Print.

3. Ryan, Brandon. *The Emotional Struggle*. Bloomington, IN: Author-House, 2007. Print.

4. Johnson, Bill. *Face to Face with God*. Lake Mary, FL: Charisma House, 2007. Print.

5. Quinion, Michael. "Cheese It!" *World Wide Words*. N.p., 25 Aug. 2007. Web. 18 Jan. 2014.

6. "Existence." *Wikipedia*. Wikimedia Foundation, 01 Feb. 2014. Web. 18 Jan. 2014.

7. Cher, and Dionne Warwick, perfs. "Alfie." By Burt Bacharach and Hal David. N.d. CD.

8. "Time Is of the Essence." *Wikipedia*. Wikimedia Foundation, 17 Nov. 2013. Web. 18 Jan. 2014.

9. "How Would You Define the Gospel?" *Church Newsletter* (Dec. 2013): n. pag. Print.

10. West, Jason B. "Now Is the Time." By Jason B. West. Rec. 2012. *Running Free*. Jason West. 2012. CD.

11. Johnson, Bill. *Dreaming with God*. Racine: Treasures Media, 2006. Print.

12. Johnson, Bill. *Strengthen Yourself in the Lord: How to Release the Hidden Power of God in Your Life*. Shippensburg, PA: Destiny Image, 2007. Print.

13. "En-." *The Free Dictionary*. Farlex, 2010. Web. 20 Jan. 2014.

14. "Root Words & Prefixes: Quick Reference." *LearnThatWord*. LearnThat Foundation, 2005. Web. 18 Jan. 2014.

15. Cooley, Lindell, and Bruce Haynes. "I Need You More." Integrity's Hosanna! Music and Centergy Music, 1996.

16. Evans, Darrell. "Trading My Sorrows." Integrity's Hosanna! Music, 1998. CD.

17. West, Jason B. *Who Will Ascend?* Omaha, NE: n.p., 2013. Print.

18. Wright, Fred, and Sharon Wright. "From Luther to Wesley: The Moravians." *The World's Greatest Revivals: How Man's Desperation Begins Waves of Revival—Including Yours*. Shippensburg, Penn.: Destiny Image, 2007. 123. Print.

Other Products Available from Anointed 2 Go MdM

Music CD

Running Free
Original Songs by Jason West
Suggested donation: $10

Books

Who Will Ascend?
Taking Prayer to Another Level
By Jason B. West
Suggested donation: $10

Downloads from Heaven
Instructions and Examples of Hearing from God
By Jay W. West
Suggested donation: $10

Willing to Yield
Discover How "Yielding" Accesses the Supernatural Wisdom, Favor, and Power of God
By Jay W. West
Suggested donation: $10

Endorsement for *Willing to Yield* by Jack Taylor:

WARNING: Do not begin reading this book unless you are willing to be distracted from what you are doing or planning to do and be arrested by and riveted to some of the greatest, most outlandish stories you have ever read! Jay West is the real thing and is one of those unique ministers to whom God entrusts varying epiphanies, or "God-happenings," as common fare.

ANOTHER WARNING: The most daring, most graphic, and most sensitive chapter is entitled, "Outmaneuvering the Manure." It may also be the most informative principle as well.

So my advice to the reader as you help yourself to these pages is, "Proceed with caution!" Do not develop an offense with the manner in which truth is articulated so as to miss the truth that might set you free!

For more information about Jack Taylor, go to his website:
http://www.jackrtaylor.com

Stay up to date with Anointed 2 Go by following Jay's blog at
http://anointed2go.com

Follow Jason's blog at **http://chroniclesofprayer.wordpress.com**

To order these and other products from Anointed 2 Go, please contact:

Jay at **anointed2go@cox.net**

or

Jason at **runningfree@cox.net**

Please note that minimal shipping costs will be added to each order, which vary slightly with each order.